100 WAYS TO IMPROVE YOUR RIDING

SUSAN McBANE

D&C
David and Charles

Opposite title page: A modern-day, exemplary classical rider and trainer Georges Dewez, riding his Lusitano stallion Nilo in piaffe.

A DAVID & CHARLES BOOK
Copyright © David & Charles Limited 2004, 2006

David & Charles is an F+W Publications
Inc. company
4700 East Galbraith Road
Cincinnati, OH 45236

Text copyright © Susan McBane 2004, 2006

Susan McBane has asserted her right to be identified as author of this work in accordance with the Copyright, Designs and Patents Act, 1988.

A catalogue record for this book is available from the British Library.

ISBN-13: 978-0-7153-1680-1 hardback
ISBN-10: 0-7153-1680-X hardback

ISBN-13: 978-0-7153-2551-3 paperback
ISBN-10: 0-7153-2551-5 paperback

Horse care and riding is not without risk, and while the author and publishers have made every attempt to offer accurate and reliable information to the best of their knowledge and belief, it is presented without any guarantee. The author and publishers therefore disclaim any liability incurred in connection with using the information contained in this book.

Printed in Singapore by KHL Printing Co Pte Ltd
for David & Charles
Brunel House   Newton Abbot   Devon

Commissioning Editor: Jane Trollope
Desk Editor: Sarah Martin
Art Editor: Sue Cleave
Project Editor: Shona Wallis
Production Controller: Jennifer Campbell

Visit our website at www.davidandcharles.co.uk

David & Charles books are available from all good bookshops; alternatively you can contact our Orderline on 0870 9908222 or write to us at FREEPOST EX2 110, D&C Direct, Newton Abbot, TQ12 4ZZ (no stamp required UK only); US customers call 800-289-0963 and Canadian customers call 800-840-5220.

Contents

Setting yourself up for success

Success is a word we hear a lot of these days but often in a context which is quite irrelevant to many people. It does not necessarily mean competitive success – it simply means that you have attained standards or goals you have set for yourself.

It is a quantum leap from not being able to get your horse out of the yard to going for an enjoyable hack in the countryside, or from being utterly overawed by dressage to realizing that you have become quite good enough to get a rosette at preliminary level.

If you ride well and your horse is well schooled, trusts your judgement and, therefore, is co-operative, you are more likely not only to be successful, but also safe because you are in reasonable control and can prevent or minimize most mishaps.

Mental attitude

In order to set yourself up for success with horses, certain things have to be borne in mind all the time:

remember what kind of animal a horse or pony is The horse is a prey animal evolved to be chased to death in open country by a predator which will give as little warning as possible. This has produced an animal which runs first and thinks later, which can get to a speed of 30mph in three or four seconds (faster than a family car) and weighs about half a ton. That's rather a sobering thought, isn't it?

horses need leadership As herd animals most horses are followers, not leaders. They are also born into an environment alien to their evolutionary one – human society – and so are not really equipped to make reasoned decisions in a man-made world, because domestication has not changed them. They speak and think in 'Horse' and behave like horses, if they have been raised with other horses and have learned equine herd manners. By assuming the role as a leader or supporter we have a great responsibility to always be fair, reliable, trustworthy and consistent, otherwise horses become confused and defensive, which can be dangerous. Ultimately, when you are together, your horse must rely on you for security, not other horses.

Conformation

Some riding problems are certainly caused because the horse simply does not have the conformation or action to perform as the rider wishes. There are several books on this topic, including my own, *Conformation for the Purpose* (Swan Hill Press, 2000). Similarly, some riders may have physical problems which make life in the saddle more difficult, but most can achieve a sufficient standard to become safe and competent enough to enjoy riding a well-mannered horse.

Take the lead

I find that most problems arise because of a lack of knowledge of effective riding techniques and a lack of a 'leader' or 'supporter' attitude when dealing with the horse. To be a good leader you must be calm, kind, firm and positive.

Equestrian tact

Up until the middle of the last century, this very meaningful phrase was often used in equestrian circles, but seems to have been lost over the years – equestrian tact. This mainly related to a rider's give-and-take attitude to horses, which can be very sensitive animals. Often 'persistent insistence' in a quiet, firm way does the trick, or a cajoling attitude can work wonders in certain situations in establishing trust, forming good habits and overcoming obstacles.

Safety through control and co-operation is essential, but the horse has a point of view which must be taken into consideration and worked with.

you must give horses clear parameters In a herd, a horse knows exactly what behaviour is acceptable and unacceptable from him to his herd-mates. If he doesn't get the same clear limits from his human counterparts, which he understands so well in nature, a horse can become spoilt, difficult and even dangerous to handle because of confusion, insecurity and lack of clear leadership. Good leadership does not mean bullying or brutality — it means love, support, guidance and, when necessary, firmness.

for safety's sake, the human has to be the senior partner
Most wise horsemen and women say that the most we can aim for is a 49/51 partnership in our favour. Much of the time the relationship may appear to be 50/50 but when the chips are down and the horse just has to do what you say when he doesn't want to, for example in a road traffic situation, he must do it for the safety of you both. Read the first point again and ask yourself if you really want to sit on that and be out of control, because if the horse doesn't do as you ask, that's what you are.

Remember: not all problems, equine and human, can be solved – but most can be improved.

Seat and weight

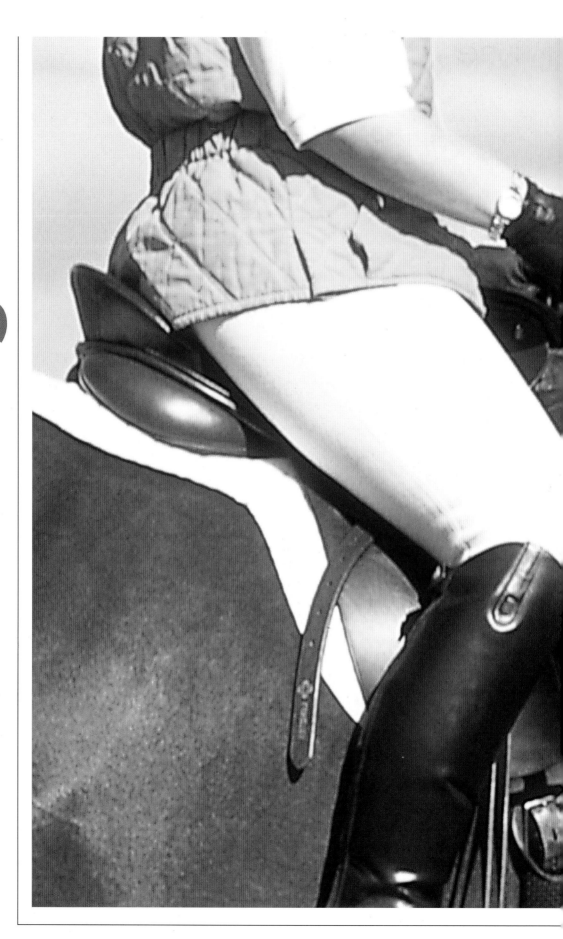

The classical seat

A good riding position will vary according to the equestrian discipline for which it is used, but all good positions are based on the traditional classical seat, including the jumping position devised in the late 19th and early 20th century by two men, Italian cavalry officer Federico Caprilli and a South American, Count Ilias Toptani, who made later refinements. The modern classical seat stipulates an upright torso and soft but 'toned' seat and legs. From the side, an onlooker should be able to drop an imaginary vertical line from the rider's ear, through the shoulder and the hip/elbow, through the ankle bone (not merely the heel) to the ground (see page 8).

To enhance that blueprint, the rider must sit up straight and gently press the back of the neck into the collar so that the ear lies above the shoulder. The rider's face should normally be directed between the horse's ears. The shoulders must be pressed gently but definitely back and down and the breastbone raised (or the ribcage expanded). The small of the back should be slightly flattened rather than arched.

The rider must sit, with an opened seat and hips, on the seatbones at the bottom of the pelvis, not back on the buttocks muscles. The seatbones or hip joints should be pushed slightly forward. The legs should be held lightly down and around the horse's sides, their weight dropping, not being pushed, down through the heel, supported via the foot which rests on its widest part along the tread of the stirrup. The ankle bone should, generally, be held beneath the seatbones and the toes should be pointed forwards as much as the rider's natural conformation permits. Clearly, the rider must use some tone (slight muscular effort) to maintain this position although once it has become second nature the effort is barely noticeable, provided the saddle is not hindering this seat through unsuitable design.

One very important refinement to this seat is that the elbows be held lightly at the hips, not several inches in front of them, as is so often seen. There should be another straight line from the rider's elbow, through the hand to the horse's mouth. The rider's forearms and the reins should, in general, form an unbroken A-shape with the horse's mouth forming the top of the A.

An ancient way of thinking can also be applied to the seat with great advantage. Those interested in eastern practices such as shiatsu, yoga, Tai Chi and in general eastern philosophy will be familiar with the concept of 'being in your centre'. The centre of the body is regarded as being inside the abdomen, a couple of inches or so below the level of the navel, which, for riding purposes, sites it just above the seatbones – ideal for the classical seat. If you can mentally and spiritually bring your awareness down from your head into your centre and ride from there, you will find that it enhances your balance, basic posture and practical effectiveness of the classical seat.

This seat has developed over many hundreds of years – having been used in war, hunting, herding, bull-fighting, tournaments and displays – confirming that it allows the best energy distribution for communicating with the horse and balancing the horse/rider unit.

Doing nothing

An eminent horseman based in the north west of England in the 1960s, Geoffrey Hattan FBHS, used to say that a rider should not be allowed to do anything until he is capable of doing nothing. He also said the most difficult thing to do on a horse is nothing. By 'nothing' he meant nothing to

interfere with the horse's movements. A rider cannot follow a horse's movements passively without doing something – and that something is moving his or her body so as to not block, but accompany, the horse, giving the impression that the rider is 'just sitting there doing nothing'. This is always a source of amazement to riders who have never been taught this principle or the technique of how to maintain a toned, 'held' torso and a loose seat and legs and to absorb the horse's movement through the small of the back and the seat.

The forward position

For modern use, adaptations for rising trot and jumping have been introduced. The upper body retains the posture described and is brought forward from the hip joints, not the waist which causes crouching, so that the shoulders are just above the knees. The seat remains in the saddle or is held lightly just above it and, in jumping all but the highest fences, the upper body is not thrown forward but folded down as if trying to touch the horse's crest with the rider's breastbone. The hands follow diagonally down the line of the shoulders to the horse's mouth during the jump.

This forward position is relevant for jumping or fast gaits, but in walk, sitting trot and canter the rider should sit upright, absorbing the movement in the seat and small of the back or loin area.

Harmony and elegance

We must aim for true lightness, balance and self-carriage of both horse and rider, for harmony and restrained elegance. Less is definitely more in classical equitation. There is no cruelty, no force – 'Nothing forced can be beautiful' Nuño Oliveira – but there is great discipline of both horse and rider. Any person who applies forceful, distressing or cruel practices to a horse is not a true classical horseman or woman, no matter what their background or how they describe themselves.

1 Using the weight aids correctly

Riding a horse that goes in complete self-carriage more-or-less entirely from your seat and weight aids is a feeling you will never forget. Executing pirouettes and flying changes or collected canter from halt and canter half-passes just by moving your seatbones and weight, with the occasional suggestion from a rein hanging by its own weight, is, as classical trainer Nuño Oliveira once exclaimed, 'the Heaven of Horsemanship'. Weight aids and, as I call them, position aids, which are even lighter, are the ultimate in physical communication with your horse only superseded by possibly the eyes and by the mind and spirit. There is no doubt that where you put your weight is where your horse will go, with hardly any exceptions.

Faulty weight distribution

Horses are sensitive to weight and position aids, and it is often the case that riders do not realize where they are putting their weight and seat. Not knowing about seat aids means that they do not control the seat and are quite innocently giving their horse a cacophony of mixed messages which can result in lumbering, uncertain responses or none at all because the horse simply can't decide what he should be doing. Some people have little natural body co-ordination and may be adamant that they are weighting one seatbone when the horse is resolutely drifting the other way because that is, in effect, where their weight is.

example Imagine a horse being asked to canter a circle to the left but who hangs right to the school entrance when he comes near. To correct this, the rider has put her left seatbone and shoulder back (instead of forward) and pulled back on the left, inside rein, making it even easier for the horse to fall out through the

RELATED AREAS OF IMPROVEMENT **15**   **34**   **39**

forward and put a bit of weight on it. Your horse will go left. Try it to the right and he will go right. Try left again but this time just position the left seatbone forward without weighting it. Your horse will go left. Try it to the right and he will go right.

My clients cannot understand why their horses comply with classical aids when they have never been schooled classically. I explain that the classical aids are based on the seat and weight and it is logical because they accord ' with how the horse uses his body.

The icing on the cake is attained when the horse will incline mentally and physically in a certain direction merely because you have 'pointed' with your seatbone, without even weighting it. Horses progressively schooled, for instance, can be taught to go into canter just by a forward positioning and lifting of the inside seatbone, keeping it forward to confirm canter to the horse as long as you want it. To return to trot, even with a green horse, you simply return the seatbone to its central (neutral) position.

outside, right shoulder. Because the horse is traversing right in a fair semblance of (unwanted) leg yield, she has let her weight go to the right (instead of left to correct it) with a view to pushing the horse over (left) from the outside (right), something I have never managed to fathom.

This is a common scenario, and there is also a school of thought which teaches that if you weight any part of your horse, this creates a block to movement because the horse can't move under the weight. But my example proves that the horse will almost always go where you put your weight, whether you want him to or not.

What can I do?

Walk on a loose rein around your school or field with your weight and seatbones centrally placed in the saddle and in the usual classical posture. Without using leg or hand, put your left seatbone

2 Developing a balanced seat

A rider's lack of balance is akin to the lack of an independent seat, the Holy Grail of horsemanship. Unlike the Holy Grail, though, it is attainable. The first step is to start thinking with your seat, not your head.

Unable to ride in harmony with the horse

Developing a balanced seat is essential in order to progress to the next stage, the independent seat we hear so much about and which is so important in all forms of riding. Without an independent seat, which means a seat which is balanced and secure no matter what the horse does underneath you, the hands cannot be used independently, either, and it is always the horse's mouth that suffers.

If the horse is not comfortable in his mouth or is constantly afraid of being jabbed in the mouth by his rider, he cannot concentrate on his work and everything the rider tries to do will be in vain.

The feeling you need to aim for is the horse's energy flowing forwards and upwards underneath you and that you are riding with your seat (which includes your thighs), weight and balance. You control his movements with your lower body, not your hands, and, being in balance, can sense those movements almost before they happen.

What can I do?

dismounted

1 **Pilates exercise:** enhances posture and balance, strengthens your core and postural (torso) muscles.

   Stand with your toes facing forwards and feet hip-width apart. Breathe in, and as you breathe out again contract upwards the internal muscles of your abdomen and pelvic floor and hold the muscle contraction while continuing to breathe. Now feel your feet firmly on the ground and lift one leg behind you a little way off the floor, keeping your thigh as vertical as possible. Imagine a long pole running vertically from the foot on the floor to the top of your head.

   Hold for 30 seconds, if you can, supporting yourself on a chair if you wobble too much, and also if you have had any kind of injury. Repeat with the other leg.

2 Make a habit of getting dressed, including underwear and socks, while standing up to make yourself balance. Also, when you get up off the floor, try to do so without holding on to anything, including your own knee!

mounted

1 Find a steady lunge horse with good rhythm in all gaits, plus either a good, classical teacher or someone who will lunge the horse and let you teach yourself by practice.

   Sit on the horse with no reins or stirrups. Hold the pommel with the inside hand to counteract centrifugal force in the faster gaits, or have a neck strap. Assume the classical position (see pages 8–9) and pretend that you have no use at all in the muscles of your seat and legs – they are completely loose and your legs are dangling, toes down naturally.

   Have the horse walk on and, looking ahead, practise sitting on your seatbones. Concentrate on keeping your torso still and stretched up above your flexible waist, soaking up the movements of your horse's back, which will dip from side to side, with your seat only. Do not let this movement rock your upper body but keep it independent above that flexible waist where all upward energy stops. You have to stay loose in the seat and hips to do this.

   Have the horse trot slowly and steadily ensuring you are absorbing the movement of sitting trot. Stay loose in the seat and legs and lean back a little. A horse with a bouncy trot is useless for you at this stage, but a good test of your absorption later. When you can balance independently, progress to canter. Again, it is essential that you keep a loose seat and legs and a 'held' torso. Rigidity or stiffness in the seat and legs provides something hard for the energy to jar against, jolting you around. Looseness soaks up that energy. You can then progress to poles, grid work and jumps, preferably with the help of a good teacher.

2 Practise standing in your stirrups at all gaits without supporting yourself by the reins. Have a neckstrap long enough to hold as you first stand up, progress a few strides at a time from halt, through walk and trot to canter. When you can canter around the school on both reins, standing up and without putting any pressure on the reins or neckstrap, you've got it.

13

3 Improving your riding posture

The pelvis is the crux of a good seat because of its facility to tilt back and forth, based on the flexing of the lumbo-sacral joint in your spine. Read page 63 for more information on how to do this correctly.

Pelvis tipped forward or back

Riding with the top of the pelvis tipped forward (and, unavoidably, the seatbones tipped back) is quite common. Most people do this because they have never been taught the benefits of a properly upright posture with the weight going directly and lightly downwards on to the seatbones. It can occur through anxiousness to allow the horse to go forward or to simply go with him. When the pelvis is tipped forwards (hollowing the back, see top right) as a matter of course, rather than momentarily to give a halt or slow-down aid, backache soon ensues! It can also cause the rider to lean forward out of balance.

Conversely, riding with the top of the pelvis tipped backwards, flattening the small of the back, causes the rider to slump in the saddle, see top left, and once again the balance is badly affected. A pelvis with the wings or 'hips' tipped too far back can simply be lack of knowledge of the correct posture, or a subconscious attempt to slow down or stop the horse.

With riders who know that a forward push of the seatbones is a request to go forward, it may be that the rider is doing this constantly to just get an apparently lazy horse to go. This pelvic position can be used as a speed-up or go-forward aid but only for a second or so, and initially accompanied by a leg aid, normally the inside leg.

What can I do?

The key to maintaining a pelvis in 'neutral', as I call it, is a knowledgeable eye on the ground. Ask a friend or teacher to take a good look at your position and posture. Once you have been put in the correct position and told that your posture is correct, get the feel of it into your consciousness and practise until it becomes second nature. It really does help to sit down lightly on the seatbones so that your weight feels as though it is falling directly, vertically down. Remember – up the body, down the legs.

4 Increasing stability when cornering and circling

The horses' natural technique when cornering at speed or on small circles is to lean in towards the centre and, left to their own devices, to turn their heads to the outside of the circle. You can see this in reining competitions, barrel racing, gymkhanas, jumping, polo and similar disciplines. Many riders experience it when riding in an arena, particularly when the horse has been asked to turn a corner or ride a circle a little smaller than he is comfortable with.

Horse and rider leaning in

A horse leaning into corners at speed is known by a few names, most commonly banking or motorbiking, and it can be dangerous apart from feeling most uncomfortable. Horses can easily lose their footing and fall, particularly on slippery going – and if they fall, you fall. Why do they lose their balance if it is their natural way of coping with tight turns? Because under saddle they have to carry a load of around a sixth of their own weight, a weight which is often not only unstable but also top heavy. They frequently just cannot balance themselves and an unpredictable rider at the same time – particularly one who leans into the turn with them.

What can I do?

This potentially dangerous fault can be rectified quite simply. The horse needs correct schooling, particularly in canter, to give him better suppleness, balance and control, while the rider needs to be able to control their own weight to help, not hinder, the horse.

The way to stop the horse banking is to sit vertically and slightly to the outside of your saddle. Do not lean in yourself thinking that you are helping the horse by following his movement. This will overbalance him and send him even further in. Sit upright with the seatbones taken slightly over to the outside and weight your outside seatbone. Your outside leg should be back slightly from the hip to encourage the horse not to swing the quarters out and weight the inside shoulder. The inside seatbone should be forward and light with the inside leg stretched long and strongly supportive down the horse's side at the girth. The inside hand should be held up to emphasize an upright inclination and to ask the horse to flex inwards.

In circumstances where the horse just has to lean in to make very tight, fast turns – sit upright as described above to counterbalance the strong inward swing of his body and to keep the pair of you on your feet, or rather his. When turning at speed, be as still and reasonably upright as you can so as not to interfere with him, and trust your horse.

5 Riding turns and circles

It is important to be clear about the classical way to turn or circle. The most effective, simple and light way to turn is to ask with the outside aids and put the inside of the body forward into the turn, moving the inside seatbone forwards. To turn right put the right side of the body forward and to turn left put the left side forward.

Collapsed hip

Riders often collapse a hip when trying to turn, or when trying to achieve a particular lateral movement – usually one which they are new to or unsure of. It is very closely related to collapsing at the waist (page 70) but in collapsing at the hip, the rider has usually mastered the upright posture of the upper body but overdoes the use of the seatbones. In a new or difficult movement, slight anxiety to get it right can take over and the rider allows the hip to drop, usually on the side away from the direction of the turn.

What can I do?

By maintaining lightness in the seat, neither hip bone should be inclined to drop or tilt. First, check your position and ensure your hips and seatbones are in a central or 'neutral' position.

To make a turn right, press the outside/left rein sideways against the neck, just in front of the withers, and take the outside leg slightly back from the hip to just behind the girth to encourage the horse to bend around the curve (so that his quarters are not swinging out but his hind feet are following along the tracks made by the forefeet). The inside seatbone, with the shoulder above it, comes forward a little with the leg at the girth and the inside hand can be slightly raised and carried slightly inwards (never backwards) to invite the horse into the turn and maintain an inward flexion. This technique of turning carries over very well to lateral work, particularly if the rider slightly lifts the inside seatbone, or the seatbone on the side to which she usually collapses.

6 Strengthening your seat to improve upper body posture

To remain secure in the saddle, one must ride in balance with the horse, maintaining a still, 'held' upper body, in all gaits, through turns and over fences. Your waist must help to absorb and softly stop the movement from your horse's back travelling up into the upper body and unbalancing it.

Leaning out when riding a circle

This fault puts the rider in an insecure position. Riders may do this if a horse makes a more sudden turn, or a tighter one, than expected, lurching the rider to the outside. It may also happen when a rider is being lunged, ideally without stirrups, and the centrifugal force pulls her to the outside and maybe off completely.

If a horse tends to track a little to the outside when circling some riders may go with him and try to get him to come in by pulling on the inside rein – this however just frees his outside shoulder and makes it easier for him to lean out, making things worse. With horses who bank or motorbike (page 15), the rider may compensate rather ineffectively by actually leaning the upper body out rather than sitting upright and moving the seat to the outside a little.

What can I do?

Be very firm with yourself about keeping your upper body erect and central. As you ride, think about keeping the centre of your chest, your breastbone, aligned with the crest of your horse's neck and your face directed between your horse's ears. Make sure that your outside stirrup is not longer than your inside one and get a friend or your teacher to check that you do not sit to the outside, drop your outside shoulder, carry your outside elbow to the outside instead of keeping it at your hip or tilt your head to the outside – all of which can, almost subconsciously, incline you towards leaning out.

7 Riding a perfect pirouette

A pirouette is a turn around the horse's inside hind leg. Horsemen devised the pirouette because it looks beautiful for display work and also because it gives excellent control of the forehand for quick turns such as getting away from a bull or an enemy. In dressage tests it is an advanced movement when requested at canter but walk pirouettes, developed from the turn on or about the haunches, are not that difficult for any rider.

Problems with pirouettes

The reason some riders and horses have difficulty with pirouettes is often because of an ineffective use of the rider's weight on the seatbone and/or stirrup. If you don't put your inside seatbone forward a little and weight it, or stretch your inside leg down which has the effect of weighting both the inside seatbone and the inside stirrup, you will get a turn of sorts but not a proper pirouette – in any gait.

What can I do?

When learning how to perform a pirouette, start by asking for just a step in the right direction. As you and your horse progress you will be able to build towards the complete movement. Start in walk until you and your horse are confident with the exercise – remember a canter pirouette is an advanced movement for the horse – both mentally and physically.

The aids, which are all part of the package, are:
1 Put your inside seatbone forward a little and weight it.
2 Put the whole of the outside leg back from the hip to stop the hindquarters swinging out, which they invariably will because the horse would rather perform his natural and easier turn on the centre.
3 Press intermittently with the outside rein on the neck just in front of the withers.
4 Keep gently asking for an inside flexion with the inside hand.

As with any new movement, or one with which you or your horse have been having problems, be delighted with even an indication that the horse is thinking of moving his forehand in the required direction. If, at your first attempt, you get a whole step, be over the moon and let your horse know it.

8 Achieving willing halts

A good halt is achieved mainly with the seat and legs with an extra suggestion from the hands. Back-up from the mind and the voice are invaluable, especially if you have been having problems. The use of the voice can be dropped later, if required.

Failure to halt in harmony

Considering so many riders call their horses lazy, it is surprising how many of them seem unwilling to halt! It is so common to see riders hauling backwards on their horses' mouths, leaning back which, in practice, pushes the horse forward, and glaring at the tops of their horse's heads at the same time. None of this will achieve a willing, light halt, in hand (on the bit) with the horse waiting to step off again at a moment's notice – which is what we should all aim to achieve.

What can I do?

use of the seat and legs Consider the following three uses of the seat to obtain a halt:

1 Slightly tighten the muscles of your buttocks and maybe the thighs, too. This lifts your seat in the saddle and prevents it moving with the movements of the horse's back. Do not be tempted to tip forward or back – sit upright. This aid is, as is any resisting aid, a powerful, psychological message to the horse that you are no longer 'with' him, making him more inclined to stop.

2 Making sure you are sitting down but lightly on your seatbones, rock forwards on them slightly, at the same time stop moving your seat with your horse's back. Again, most horses will stop for this aid, particularly in combination with voice and a resisting, *not pulling*, hand.

3 Ride along with your pelvis in 'neutral' (see page 14), then slightly push your seatbones back by tilting the pelvis (hollowing your back slightly), sitting upright and ceasing to move with the horse's back. Again, voice and hand in support should achieve a good halt.

use of the hands The use of the hands in halt is most definitely NOT to pull backwards. The fingers should gently but unmistakably close on the reins and stop moving with the movements of the horse's head, thereby resisting rather than pulling. This, combined with the seat aid and a voice command the horse already understands such as 'stand' or 'whoa', will bring most horses to halt without raising their head or pulling. If the horse does resist, tap sideways with the inside leg to send him forward into the hand and intermittently give and take with the fingers on the inside rein to destabilize the bit against which he is pulling and ask him to relax his jaw and lower his head. Once relaxed ask for another halt.

9 Improving your jumping position

As a horse takes off over a jump the rider should fold the upper body down from the hip joints. Folding down over the horse like this is an effective, balanced and economical movement for the rider and minimizes disruption to the horse's balance.

Failure to fold down when jumping

The old saying 'throw your heart over the fence and your horse will follow' is true to a large extent. Unfortunately, it can be easily misinterpreted as a potentially dangerous physical action – that of throwing the upper body too far forward at take-off. A few years ago the British eventing world did a survey and analysis into falls and accidents in competition and it was found that most falls occur because riders get in front of the movement and so are more easily unseated, usually forwards, if problems ensue. As a result, riders are now taught not to lean too far forward and to keep their weight over the horse's centre of gravity.

What can I do?

When approaching your fence, be in a jumping seat with your stirrups at a comfortable jumping length. Lean forward from the hip joints – not the waist – keeping your back flat and your shoulders pushed gently back and down. If they drop forward it will affect your balance and self-control.

At take-off, lower your breastbone to your horse's crest by folding down and closing the hip joints, and push your seat back a little. Keep your lower legs vertical and down throughout the whole jump letting your weight drop through your loose ankles. As the horse descends and lands, your upper body should automatically return to position.

As your horse stretches his head and neck over the jump let your hands go diagonally down your horse's shoulders and forward towards his mouth, keeping the elbow-hand-horse's mouth straight line. Taking the hands up the crest towards the ears, as so often seen, doesn't 'lift' the horse but can raise the rider's upper body and shorten the rein at the very time when the horse needs complete freedom of his head and neck.

21

Seat and weight

10 Improving your balance when jumping

A jump has five phases – approach, take-off, flight, landing and the get-away. The actual jump is not finished until the horse is in the get-away phase. It is therefore important to stay in balance with the horse throughout all phases at every jump you tackle.

Landing heavily after a jump

Landing heavily in the saddle can occur because the rider is so relieved to have got over the jump that he or she gets back into the upright position too soon, or the rider may be anxious to prepare for the next fence and is unconsciously rushing the process. This fault can be a cause of horses dropping their hind legs over a fence in anticipation of a bang on the back on landing, and also of the horse bucking and charging off on landing for the same reason. Anything uncomfortable to the horse while jumping, such as a bang on the back or a jab in the mouth, can also cause run outs and refusals.

What can I do?

Steadily canter your horse on a fairly long rein, so you've no chance of using it to balance yourself but feel that you have some control, over undulating (not rough) ground, such as a ridge and furrow field, or any reliable ground with gentle dips and rises. Stand lightly in your jumping position (see page 20) with your seat almost brushing the saddle, be in good balance with your lower leg vertical and feel that your

horse is pivoting around your knee joint. Keep the knee soft and imagine a rod running through the horse from knee to knee around which the horse may pivot but you may not.

Once you can stay balanced, progress to riding in the same way over raised poles or tiny fences, then slightly

higher ones. As the fences increase in height, think of keeping your seat up out of the saddle (legs down) on landing and think ahead until the horse is completely on the flat and trotting or cantering in the get-away phase and beyond. To improve your balance overall, try the exercises on page 13.

11 Improving your sitting trot

When riding a sitting trot correctly, a rider absorbs the energy coming up from the horse's back into the seat and waist without letting it travel any further up the body. To perform this correctly it is crucial that you not only keep your upper body erect and 'held' (but not stiff), but also that your seat and legs are completely relaxed. Only in this way can you soak up the energy and dissipate it.

Bouncing about in sitting trot

As an equine shiatsu therapist as well as a classical riding teacher, I am sure that many cases of bruised backs are due to riders banging down on them (despite well-fitting saddles) in sitting trot.

What can I do?

Try to get access to a steady lunge horse with smooth gaits and have some sessions in trot, without stirrups or reins, to improve your seat and position. Imagine that you are gently but firmly stuck to your saddle with glue all over the seat of your jodhpurs. If the horse will jog, although most are firmly discouraged from doing so, this will help bring you into the technique gradually. Next progress to a slow, but active trot and finally on to a horse with a bouncy trot – all on the lunge.

Concentrate on 'glueing' your seat to the saddle by allowing the small of your back to gently move backwards and forwards, flattening and hollowing as the horse rises and lands, respectively, in trot. Look ahead and feel this with your seat rather than looking down at your horse, which reduces your sensitivity. The combination of the 'glue' and the looseness of the legs will enable you to really sit to the trot with practice. Stay focused and relaxed in your mind and once you've felt this soft, absorbing sitting trot, believe me you will never look back – and your horse will be so relieved.

RELATED AREAS OF IMPROVEMENT · 2 · 32 · 38

12 Improving your rising trot

There are variations of opinion on the classical way to ride a rising trot, however I find that the most effective way is for the back to remain flat as the rider brings the upper body forward from the hip joints, carrying the shoulders above the knees. In this position, the rise is much lessened and can be done subtly by just tilting the bottom of the pelvis forwards on one trot diagonal and letting it come back again (sitting lightly) on the next. There is no pushing up from the legs, which should be consciously dropped on the rise.

By riding in this way, you are not performing an up-and-down movement but a forward-and-sit one. This method of rising trot is only a knack and you will get it if you give yourself time and keep reminding yourself not to rise, but to tilt the pubic bone and seatbones forward instead. In fact, I like to call this a forward trot rather than a rising trot to encourage the correct movement. As you sit, tuck your bottom under you a little which will neaten your movement in the saddle even more.

Rising too high

I often come across this problem because people seem to have been taught that they must sit upright in rising trot and execute a 'clear rise'. This method of rising trot has a lot of disadvantages which should be understood. The hands and arms very often go up and down the same distance as the upper body. The rider may well be trying to keep her hands

RELATED AREAS OF IMPROVEMENT   22   32   50

still, but they are usually kept still in relation to the rider's body – whereas they need to be kept still in relation to the horse's mouth, which stays fairly level in trot. If the rider's balance is poor, the reins may even be used as an anchor, increasing the horse's discomfort.

The amount of thrust that some people put into rising trot very often causes stiff ankles and raised heels as the rider pushes up with every stride. These are usually accompanied by lower legs and feet which flap out and in again as the rider rises and sits. The horse feels this as a leg aid at every stride and may whizz around far too fast or, conversely, simply ignore it, giving the false impression that he is by nature dull or lazy.

What can I do?

Think of not being able to raise your upper body, keeping your shoulders under rails running immediately above them. Use the brim of your riding hat as a gauge of your effectiveness: pick a landmark ahead of you and watch to see if the brim is rising and falling in relation to it. If it is, so are you.

Rising forward instead of up also makes it much easier for the rider to keep the hands still in relation to the horse's mouth, her balance will be easier to keep, she will not flap her legs and everyone will be happier all round. As you rise to the trot, drop and relax your legs and feet down and round the horse rather than pushing up with them, tilt the lower part of your pelvis forward, then allow it to return to 'neutral' as you sit lightly.

Stay relaxed and the movement of the horse will lift you up slightly as you go forward – it's up to you to control this and go forward instead of too far up. Slightly flatten the small of your back as you move forward and return it to normal as you sit.

Some riders, as they sit after rising, raise the knee and heel. This is usually because they are not in balance and are allowing the upper body to rock backwards as they sit and the lower leg to go forwards. It is also a sign of a stiff leg and of not thinking about the legs being draped around the horse's sides like two wet tea towels, that are stuck there by surface tension, not grip. Think always of dropping your relaxed legs down and around the horse's body, almost as though you are trying to get your feet to meet under his breastbone.

13 Recognizing the correct trot diagonal

Trot is a two-time, diagonal gait with a moment of suspension after each step. The legs move in diagonal pairs like this – left hind and right fore together, then right hind and left fore together with the moment of suspension between each pair. To ride on the correct diagonal, a rider must rise when the horse's outside shoulder is going forward and sit when the outside shoulder is back. When riding in a straight line or when hacking it doesn't matter which diagonal you rise and sit to as long as you change frequently to avoid producing uneven muscle development and balance in the horse.

The incorrect diagonal

Many riders find it difficult to tell which trot diagonal they are rising on without leaning forwards and looking down at their horse's shoulders to check. However, it is not necessary to look once you have learned how to 'feel'.

What can I do?

We use the horse's shoulders as a guide to whether or not we are correct because they are easy to see if we glance down to check. If the shoulder is moving forward or back so must its foreleg, and so must the opposite hind leg. So if the rider rises when the outside shoulder and foreleg go forward, she is also up when the inside hind leg is forward, which means she is on the correct diagonal. The present theory behind why we rise on this diagonal is that this leaves the inside hind leg (which does most of the pushing) free to come forward unencumbered by the rider's weight so encouraging free, forward movement – provided that the rider isn't restricting the horse with the reins.

It is possible to feel the correct diagonal, eliminating the need to look down and risking unbalancing yourself and your horse. As a horse's hind foot comes forward, the same side of his back will dip and, because the trot is a diagonal gait, the opposite shoulder/foreleg will come forward simultaneously. By riding with a relaxed seat in sitting trot, the rider should be able to feel this dip thus enabling them to go into rising trot on the correct diagonal without looking down to check. Spend some time feeling your horse's hind legs moving forwards underneath you in walk. Then progress to a slow, active, sitting trot. Loosen your seat and leg muscles. When you feel the outside hind come forward (and the inside shoulder), rise on the next beat and carry on from there and you will be on the correct diagonal.

14 Strengthening your cross-country seat

For a horse and rider to successfully negotiate solid fences and ride across undulating terrain at speed, the rider must first be able to maintain a balanced forward position with the stirrups at jumping length, before even considering approaching a jump. These basics will enable the horse to stay in balance, lighten the load he has to carry and prepare both the horse and rider for cross-country jumping.

Unable to maintain cross-country position

A lack of physical strength in the upper body and legs, coupled with a lack of balance, are the common causes of riders being unable to support their weight when riding in a forward position. Common problems include balancing on the horse's neck or the reins, tipping forwards or bouncing in the saddle and general rider fatigue.

What can I do?

By improving your overall balance in the saddle, see page 13 for riding exercises, you will also gradually and indirectly improve your strength. Enquire at your local gym about a strengthening programme – squats and forward lunges are great for strengthening leg and buttock muscles while lying on your front on the floor and

carefully lifting your head and shoulders up slightly strengthens the back.

Practise riding with your weight out of the saddle progressing to work over trotting poles. Start with just one pole and build up to a grid of six, ensuring the distance between the poles is correct for your horse's stride length. Approach the poles in a rising trot. As you reach the poles stay up on the rise and let your weight drop down through your heels and relaxed ankles. Do not rely on your reins for balance. Once you can trot over a row of six poles without tipping forwards or resting your hands on the horse's neck, progress to grid work with a small fence at the end. After you have mastered this you can go on to tackle small obstacles on undulating ground. Concentrate on keeping your seat just above the saddle and on dropping your legs around the horse.

Steady, frequent work like this will both strengthen you and improve your horse's technique in a few weeks.

15 Improving your position in canter

The canter is called a diagonal gait and it is the only gait which gives the rider a sensation of rocking vertically up and down and also back and forth. Imagine the horse in mid-air in the moment of suspension with his four legs tucked underneath him. He is in right canter so his left hind will come forward and down first. As it lands, his hindquarters lower and his back, forehand, head and neck will be felt to come up and slightly back towards the rider. They level as his right hind and left fore land, and lower as his leading leg, the right fore, lands. At that point, too, the hindquarters rise a little allowing the hind legs to come forward. Then, when the leading leg leaves the ground, all his legs tuck up underneath his body again in the next suspension phase – and the sequence is repeated.

Rocking back and forth in canter

Many riders, sitting on that rocking sensation, instinctively try to counteract the up-and-down-back-and-forth thrust of the horse's body. Without thinking, they let their upper body go forwards (to prevent themselves being thrown back) as the outside/left hind lands and the forehand lifts towards them, and backwards again when the leading/right leg lands (to avoid being thrown forwards and down) and the forehand drops – so they are rocking against the horse's movements, counterbalancing themselves which is understandable, but wrong!

What can I do?

Order yourself to sit up straight and absorb the movement of the horse with your seat, mainly through your hips, although the spine comes into play as well. Imagine that your seatbones and hip joints form a hinge between your seat and your horse's back. The hinge is set across the saddle, one flap of the hinge going up as your body and the other lying flat as the horse's body. To avoid rocking, you must let the lower half of the hinge rock up and down but the upper half keep vertical, so only the lower half of the hinge is moving.

To help, think of the horse rocking up and down beneath the fulcrum of your seatbones but supplement this with a slight forward movement of your upper body (from the seatbones/hips hinge) as the leading leg lands (opposite to your natural tendency to rock backwards at this point), and of allowing your upper body to return to vertical – not rocking backwards – as the outside hind lands for a new stride.

Hands and arms

Developing good hands

Good hands – an old-fashioned term overdue for revival – are hands the horse can trust to inform, guide and request, and trust to not hurt. They are quiet, listening, polite and responsive hands which can be firm or gentle, but always just.

An extremely common fault is a rider using the reins to keep his or her balance in the saddle. This is entirely due to an insecure seat and a lack of realization that the reins are not there for security but for communication. Another fault is hard, unrewarding hands – that is, hands which do not give and say 'thank you' when the horse does what the hands are asking. As in all training, if the horse receives no reward by release of even slight pressure, he will never understand what you are asking because he gets no response, and therefore has no reason to comply.

The greatest classical rider of the 20th century, the Portuguese master Nuño Oliveira, advised: 'When the horse takes, you take. When the horse gives, you give.' Take means resist *not* pull. Many riders use too much hand and not enough seat. A rider must learn to sense when a horse is taking the rein, also when he is giving and working within the parameters you have set.

A little give and take

You may find taking and giving easier if you hold and use the reins in the following way: Concentrate on holding the part of the reins which comes up the inside of your hand and out between your thumb and index finger mainly by pressure from your thumb on the middle bone of your index finger. This means that you have your bottom three fingers available to 'talk' down the reins and to close (take) or open (give), as appropriate. You can take or give two or three inches by using this technique without moving your elbow from its position at your hip.

When the horse is taking, you will feel a fairly firm, even hard, pressure on one or both reins. When you need to take the rein, this is done not by pulling back as is so often seen, but by keeping your elbow firmly at your hip, not letting the horse draw it forward and not letting the rein run through your hand. This is usually best done with the outside rein. With your inside rein, take and give intermittently as much as necessary to get the horse to respond to your rein aid and stop taking. Most importantly, always accompany your rein aid with your inside leg by intermittent squeezes or taps immediately behind the girth (which some people call on the girth). When the horse gives, remember, you must give, too.

the handshake test Here is a good way to help you learn to judge 'good hands' and the pressure of appropriate contact. If you are introduced to someone and you shake hands, the weakness or strength of their grip gives you a good idea of what kind of personality they have – weak, sloppy and unreliable; firm and confident but gentle and trustworthy; or hard, stiff, gripping and controlling. The middle type of handshake is the one we'd all prefer. Now think about this:

If you were blind, which person would you trust to hold your hand and help you cross the road?
Which person would you not trust to lead you through a critical situation?
And which person, or people, would you not want to spend your life with?

If you consider these handshakes when you are riding your horse and think of 'holding his hand' mainly with your outside rein, this will help you gauge a contact which the horse is likely to trust.

16 Establishing the correct hand position

A good, general guideline for the correct hand position is to hold your hands so that from the side view there is a straight line from the rider's elbow (which should normally be back at the hip) through the hand to the horse's mouth. From above, form an A-shape with the forearms and reins. The horse's mouth and bit form the top of the A and the elbows, the base. The hands should be between the two on a straight line so that the branches of the A are not broken inward or outward. This is a good base position which can be used when things are going smoothly or if the rider is in doubt. Educated riders will certainly momentarily move the hands according to what seems necessary to communicate a particular effect to the horse – upwards, downward, together, apart, sideways or forwards.

Inappropriate hand position

It is often difficult for riders to decide just where to hold their hands on different horses. If both hands are carried too low on a horse going correctly, it may, depending on the horse, have the effect of causing the head to be raised too high (usually blood-type horses) or dropped too low (chunkier types – as in the photo right). If both hands are held too high, it can, depending on the horse's individual reaction, cause the head to tilt downward or to come up with the muzzle poking out (see photo top right).

Many riders are tempted to pull backwards in an attempt at control. Although we must all have done this in the past you will have noticed that pulling directly back on the horse's mouth doesn't really work, causing more problems and resistances elsewhere in the body. The horse will often pull harder and his mouth could become injured. Then his head may go up beyond the point of control – or some horses may bring the muzzle

backwards towards the chest, thus going overbent. If the horse can still not avoid this discomfort, he may begin to 'snake' any way he can. If he is actually galloping – which may be the reason for the backward pull – he will usually just go even faster.

What can I do?

As a general rule, it is usually best to keep the hand on the outside rein in the straight-line, base position and to vary the inside hand/rein as needed. For instance, when turning, keep the outside hand level with the withers and slightly raise the inside one, possibly also opening it a little. A light, intermittent, sideways pressure of the outside rein immediately in front of the withers can greatly assist a turn. Remember, never pull the horse round with the inside rein but push from the outside rein and leg for better, more balanced, results.

Green and novice horses, however, should be encouraged to work in a long and low shape with the muzzle out in front and the head a little lower than the horse might carry it naturally. This encourages him to stretch his topline and raise his belly and back into a strong, safe, weight-carrying posture. He will also come to realize that it is more comfortable and effective to bring the hindquarters and hind legs forward and under. The hands will, in this case, be about level with the withers, maintaining the straight line of elbow-hand-horse's mouth.

We often see the hands held rather high on highly-schooled riding horses, such as those competing in Grand Prix or sometimes Prix St. George level dressage. This is due to the higher head (and therefore mouth) position achieved by such horses who are capable of going in true collection, with the neck and head raised, the poll at the highest point and the front of the face on the vertical or very slightly in front of it.

33

17 Improving your wrist position

The ideal wrist position is simply to keep the wrist straight and in line with the hand and forearm, and vertical so that the thumb is on top and the little finger underneath. Of course, there are times when you need to flex your wrists slightly, for example to move your hands with the movements of the horse's head in walk without moving your elbows backwards and forwards.

Faulty wrist positions

When we think of the correct hand position when riding, we think of straight lines from bit to elbow, as described on pages 32 and 33, however these straight lines and direct contact down the reins can be easily disturbed and broken by wrists bending in various incorrect directions:

'pram' wrists A common problem where riders hold the wrists horizontally as if they are pushing a pram or typing (see top photo). Try riding like this for a little while, then ride with the wrists vertical, and you are almost sure to notice how much more sensitive your hands and rein contact are in the second position.

bent wrists Riding with the wrists bent in any direction (breaking the straight line from elbow to horse's mouth) is often a sign of tension and anxiety (see bottom photo).

over-long reins The rider may be trying to compensate for over-long reins without wanting to shorten them. This is a fault many people have because they either misunderstand lightness and going on the weight of the rein, they feel that it is unkind to pull on the reins, the horse will not accept a contact or perhaps his mouth is sore and needs attention.

What can I do?

To keep your hands and wrists in the correct position, imagine you are holding a hock glass (long-stemmed wine glass) with the stem running down the centre of each hand, and that it contains your favourite tipple! You have to keep each glass upright or you will spill the wine. To reduce tension in your wrists consider relaxation techniques such as yoga, meditation, aromatherapy, Alexander Technique or Feldenkrais, which can all be of help.

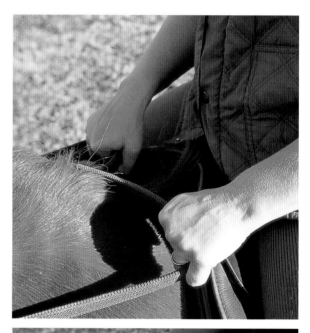

18 Riding with relaxed hands

A rider needs to hold the reins as if holding the hand of a toddler – the hold needs to be gentle and comforting, yet firm enough to control the child. Some teachers suggest that you should use the same amount of force as you would use to hold a small bird in your hand – enough to prevent it flying away but not enough to frighten or hurt it.

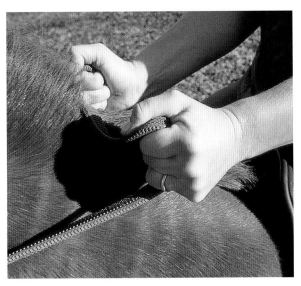

Clenched hands

Anxiety and fear may manifest itself as tension within the rider particularly as clenched fists (photo above) or hunched shoulders. Clenching the hands can also be a sign of insensitivity or lack of feel on the part of the rider, or may even occur through a lack of balance such as an insecure seat.

What can I do?

The first thing to do is discover the cause of the problem – is it fear, tension, a lack of balance or a feeling of being over-horsed? Clenched fists due to a lack of balance through an insecure seat can usually be put right by having lessons on the lunge using a steady, reliable horse with rhythmic, steady gaits. The best way to be lunged is without stirrups and reins, holding a neckstrap or the pommel at first, and to be taught to completely relax the seat and legs. Being lunged can also help overcome the nerves and help build a rider's confidence and self-belief.

If the problem is that of being over-horsed, but the horse is your own, try having lessons on a more suitable horse for a while and consider allowing a more confident and competent rider to school your horse. Once you have confidence in your ability you could start to have lessons on your own horse. However, if the horse is very unsuitable, it may be wise to find a steadier horse on a permanent basis.

A useful exercise to solve clenched fists is to ride around holding the reins mainly between the thumb and the middle bone of the index finger and to fully open out the bottom three fingers of each hand, to show yourself that you really don't need to grip. Close the fingers lightly around the rein. Next open one hand, then the other. Close again around the rein and so on, until you are convinced about the lack of needing to grip. Even if you clench your fists unconsciously, riding this exercise will create a new pattern for your body and you will eventually loosen your hold naturally.

19 Achieving smoother turns

To ride a perfect turn you must first understand the correct aids and their application. To make a turn to the right, move your right seatbone forward a little, hold your inside (right) rein slightly into the turn and/or give a slight feel or squeeze on it by tightening your fingers a little and press your outside (left) rein sideways, immediately in front of the wither, supporting with the outside leg slightly back.

Hands crossing horse's neck when turning

Having absorbed the fact that it is better to 'push' the horse around a turn with the outside aids than to pull him with the inside rein, the rider often allows the outside hand to go forward and up to allow the horse to flex into the turn (followed logically by the elbow and sometimes by the upper body) and then brings the outside hand over the neck in an anxious attempt to get the turn. All this destroys the rider's position and changes the rein contact with the bit. It can also happen because the rider is not using enough, or correct, seat and leg aids and so feels the need for too much rein to compensate.

Sometimes the problem is with the inside rein if the rider is not used to using an open rein (holding the rein a little sideways, not pulling it backwards, into the turn), or because the inside rein is too long. The inside hand crosses over the withers, often with the wrist bending towards the rider's tummy, in a futile effort to take up the rein.

RELATED AREAS OF IMPROVEMENT · **20** **28** **70**

What can I do?

To prevent yourself getting into a mess, remember the straight lines and A-shape patterns (see page 32), and say to yourself 'left rein on the left side, right rein on the right side' to help you keep them there. If all else fails, and you keep crossing your hands, imagine an electric wire running down the crest of the horse's neck to the pommel of your saddle. That should help!

In the photograph on the right, the rider's hands are nicely separated, although it shows what can happen if there is even a little too much tension on the inside rein on a horse with a light mouth. It can cause an exaggerated bend in the head and neck which, in turn, can make it easy for the horse to 'fall out' of the bend to the outside.

Here, in the bottom photo, is a really nice curve to the left as the horse starts to come off the track. The rider has put her inside seatbone forward and is inviting the horse into the turn by bringing her lightly held inside rein sideways, not backwards, to the left. This confirms the direction to the horse and encourages a soft flexion – just enough – to the left, whilst he steps well under with his inside hind to push around the curve.

20 Maintaining the correct rein length

A good, well-schooled riding horse should move in self-carriage (collected balance and controlled posture independent of support from the rider) and on the weight of the rein. Surely, 'on the weight of the rein' means no contact? Well, no. It might mean no pressure, but it doesn't mean no contact for communication. Even on a loose rein, the horse can feel a swing, vibration or re-positioning of the rein.

If the horse's schooling progresses correctly, his body gradually becomes stronger, his posture easy to maintain, he grows lighter in the hand and able to go, indeed, 'in self-carriage on the weight of the rein'. Until that time, we need to help him find his way into this by means of a rein length which will support him without either constricting or abandoning him.

Inappropriate rein length

Why is the correct rein length important? The answer is simple: to give a green or moderately-schooled horse the right amount of 'space' to work in to encourage him to learn to work in a good posture which is slightly shortened from back to front – and this will (almost) never happen if he is not set a fair boundary by means of the reins. If the reins are too short the horse will either lean on the bit, pull against the rider or drop behind the contact (overbent). If the reins are too long the horse will never arch his head and neck up and forward into a guiding, sympathetic contact, raise his back and belly and thrust forward from lowered hindquarters.

What can I do?

To help gauge the correct length and feel on the reins, think of it as if you were holding the horse's hand with the outside rein to produce a comfortable feel for both parties. The support and space is given mainly with the outside hand and rein which remain steady and still, maintaining an even contact with the mouth as the head moves naturally in the different gaits.

Down the inside rein, the rider gives intermittent, give-and-take squeezes to ask the horse to accept the bit by flexing vertically a little at the poll, and slightly opening the joints just below the ears where the lower jaw is attached to the skull. This allows him to give to the bit – something he cannot do without opening his mouth slightly, therefore the noseband must allow room for this. The rider asks for hind leg activity and thrust by means of intermittent taps or squeezes with the inside leg (or, if necessary, both legs) and/or a rhythmic forward lifting of the seat. It is sometimes difficult for a rider to know when her horse is overbent (as in the bottom photo on page 38), whether the horse has overbent of his own accord or the rider has encouraged this by too short a rein.

Ask your teacher or a knowledgeable friend to watch you riding round and to tell you the instant the horse's face comes behind the vertical. If your inside rein contact, particularly, is too firm, open your fingers and be softer in the hand. If you are certain that your rein contact is not overpowering, tap or intermittently squeeze with your inside leg to ask the horse to go up to his bit. Look at the posture of his neck from your view in the saddle when the horse is both correct and overbent. Remember: the slight nuance in change will enable you to judge the situation on your own in future.

21 Developing sympathetic hands

It is effective and also acceptable to the horse for the rider to use the outside rein mainly for speed control, assisting with bends and to support the horse in his efforts to find the right posture, and to use the inside rein for requests to give to the bit, and to deliver little vibrations or feels for a myriad of requests.

Beginner riders have to learn and try their best to develop good hands. In their early days, their hands may well be a little rough because they have not developed the co-ordination, balance and independence of body and seat which enables the hands to perform their purpose of communicating with the horse. As their equestrian education moves on, any good teacher will be able to tell whether or not the rider is developing good hands.

Harsh hands

If there is one thing a rider must try to avoid having, it is harsh hands. These are hands that stab and yank on the reins unnecessarily; pull backwards relentlessly; apply too hard a contact for the action taking place; keep up a firm contact without let-up or relief for the horse and are hands that cannot sense when the horse needs more freedom and less restriction. They are hands which, in a hard, blunt way, tend both to do the same thing at the same time rather than acting separately but still in harmony. Many riders find it very hard to do one thing with one hand and a different thing with the other.

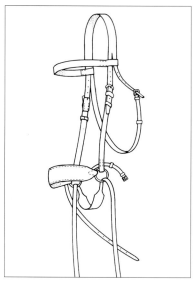

What can I do?

You may find it useful to read the introduction to this section again before reading on. Remember that a lack of an independent seat can also cause bad hands as the rider will use the reins as lifelines to help stay in balance – or even just on board.

If you feel you use your hands too much or too harshly, consider going right back to basics. Enlist the

help of a sympathetic instructor to help you develop a lighter way of riding. Invest in some lunge lessons to ensure you can ride completely independently of the reins.

If it seems that you don't have natural sensitivity in this department, and are having difficulty in acquiring it, it may be a good idea to fit your horse with a soft rubber or rubber-coated snaffle bit.

It is better by far to have what are termed as 'no hands' – hands which do nothing and don't exert any influence

on the horse – than to have heavy, busy, cruel, mutton-fisted or insensitive hands. You might consider riding mainly out of touch as far as the horse's mouth is concerned. A generous, quiet and well-balanced horse who knows his job can manage with this style quite well. Such a horse also might be a good candidate for being ridden in a Scawbrig bitless bridle (see illustration) or any type of bitless bridle which does not work by means of exerting leverage – these needing just as sensitive handling as a curb bit.

22 Using your hands independently of your body

It is vital to acquire a secure and independent seat without reliance on the reins if a rider wishes to become truly competent.

A rider must develop the ability not only to treat the hands as separate from the rest of the body, but also as independent of the horse's mouth, rather than always accompanying his head movement, such as when an aid or request is necessary to get the horse to do something opposite to what he clearly wants or intends to do. Safety must be our first priority (riding being a risky enough sport as it is) and there are admittedly times when a strong contact is needed for control or with a difficult, recalcitrant horse. As soon as things improve, the hands can become gentle again to reward the horse.

Catching the horse in the mouth

We all make mistakes and cannot entirely predict what a horse is going to do with his body, but involuntary movements of our own bodies and hands can be minimized if we ride habitually from our centres (see below). Catching the horse in the mouth is primarily due to an insecure seat, affecting riders who have not grasped the knack of keeping the action of the hands separate from that of the body. Even experienced riders, however, can remain dependent on their hands, not merely to keep their balance, but in an effort to control their horse (and some can be really harsh in doing this) whereas this ought to be done with the seat, weight and legs.

What can I do?

If you can think in terms of dropping your awareness down into your centre of gravity or mass, the area below your tummy button, between your hips and just above your seatbones, you will find that you become much more able and inclined to ride from your seat. Think of this area, which is called your 'centre' in eastern practices such as yoga, shiatsu, Tai Chi and so on, as where it all comes from. Your centre is in direct touch with your horse's body and legs which produce energy and direction. Keep your seat opened across your horse's back/saddle, rest lightly, with your legs relaxed and dropped down and round your horse's ribcage, staying there almost by surface tension, like two wet tea towels.

If you practise, you will soon find that this seat and philosophy actually 'detach' your hands from your balance – you don't need them other than for directing energy, asking the horse to give to the bit, helping to control speed and bends and, most importantly, allowing forward movement on the flat and giving him space to use his head freely when jumping without fear of pain or restriction.

Hands and arms

23 Improving your ability with double reins

A double bridle, comprising a thin bridoon (bradoon or snaffle) and a curb bit of varying kinds, has long been regarded by true horsemen as the epitome of bitting arrangements as you can obtain the finest nuances of communication and effect with your horse.

Another bit which uses double reins is the pelham – a bit in which many horses go beautifully, particularly those who simply don't have room in their mouths for two bits, although it is currently banned from competitive dressage. A pelham can be used with a single rein by fitting roundings – rounded pieces of leather which attach, one on each side, to the bridoon ring and the curb ring, then a single rein attaches to the rounding on each side. Personally I dislike roundings because they offer no differentiation between snaffle and curb action – you can't get away from either and would be far better using a Kimblewick.

Inability to hold and use double reins

It is a good plan to persevere with using double reins because, once you reach the more advanced levels of riding, not only in competition, you can obtain more subtlety in your aids and your horse's responses with a double bridle and also with the wrongly-maligned pelham. Also, at lower levels, some horses and ponies just don't cooperate very well with a snaffle and a correctly-used pelham can achieve lightness quicker and more effectively.

What can I do?

I find that the main problem with holding and using double reins lies in the rider's head simply because it has been put there by today's attitude to them in some quarters. At least in the UK, a culture has grown up which not only claims that double reins (in other words, bits other than snaffles) are not only unnecessary but actually show that the rider cannot control the horse in a snaffle and must, therefore, be a bad rider. What rubbish! People who believe this should perhaps reflect on the original purpose of snaffle bits – they were invented for grooms, novices and the mutton-fisted!

If you want to learn how to use double reins correctly, the only answer is practice – ideally with a sympathetic teacher. Begin by riding with the curb rein hanging quite loose (as in photo above) so you won't be frightened of hurting the horse. It is amazing how he will respond to it even if you don't use it directly. Experiment with different ways of holding the reins (see next page) and discover what works best for you and your horse.

Holding double reins

There is no right or wrong way to hold the reins, single or double. The best way to hold the reins is the one which suits you and the horse you are riding and which gives you the best results. The ability to use double reins sensitively, fairly and effectively is a sign of an educated and skillful rider.

The most usual way to hold double reins today is to cross them and have the bridoon (snaffle) rein under the ring finger and the curb rein between the second and third finger (see above). One reason for using this method is that the bridoon is still under the ring finger as it is when holding a snaffle, so is familiar for those getting used to double reins. Also, if needed, you have a firm hold in a method with which you are fairly familiar and the curb is between your two weaker fingers so is unlikely to be used too strongly.

Personally, I find it difficult to use and adjust each rein independently with the reins crossed and prefer the way in which I was taught as a child (below). The bridoon is held between the index or first finger and the middle or second finger and the curb between the ring or third finger and the little or fourth finger. This hold is logical as the top rein is attached to the top bit (the bridoon) and the bottom rein to the bottom bit (the curb). This logic works just as well in practice whether you are using two bits as with a double bridle or one bit as with a pelham. The reins are separated by two fingers so are clearly apart both in your hands and in your mind, and are easy to use independently of each other. The bridoon is under a strong finger and the curb under a weaker one so if you need to 'take a hold' you can, but can leave the curb out of the equation simply by opening your ring finger.

Other methods of holding double reins are usually a variation on this method, the reins being moved up or down a finger or sometimes separated by only one finger, according to the rider's preference. There is nothing to stop you changing the positions of the reins as you ride according to you and your horse's requirements, for as subtle an effect as possible commensurate with safety and control.

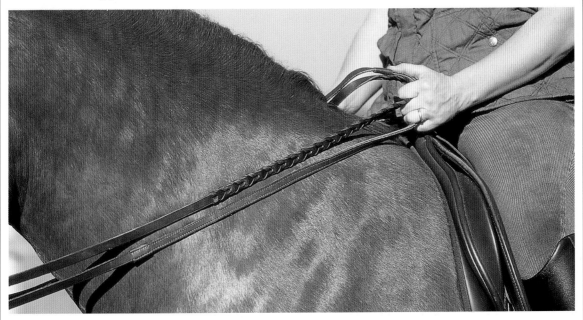

24 Using the curb chain more effectively

The curb arrangement of a double bridle, pelham or Kimblewick works by exerting a grip on the lower jaw from both inside and outside the horse's mouth – namely the bars and chin groove. This sounds awful but, executed very lightly, a trained horse will respond by opening his lower jaw slightly and giving or flexing to the bit. There is also some downward pressure on the poll via the curb bit's headstall, exerted by the upper cheek of the bit which goes forwards and downward as the lower cheeks are drawn backwards by the reins.

Poor use of the curb chain and rein

Many people either adjust their curb chains too loosely (top photo) because they feel that this is kinder to their horse, or too tightly for control (middle photo) – neither of which works at all well in practice.

What can I do?

Learn to fit the bridle and curb chain correctly. A jointed bit (snaffle or bridoon) should cause one wrinkle at the corners of the lips unless the horse puts his tongue over it or a male horse's tushes touch it – in both cases no more than two wrinkles are permissible. The curb bit of a double bridle, however, should lie just below the bridoon and so does not touch the corners of the lips. A non-jointed bit such as a Kimblewick or pelham – both of which have a chain, should touch the corners of the lips without wrinkling them.

A curb chain acts by tightening in the horse's chin groove when the lower cheeks of the curb bit form an angle of no more than 45 degrees with the line of the lips. When fitting a curb chain you should always be able to run a finger under the chain between it and the chin groove. When correctly adjusted, you need to apply no more than the hint of a squeeze or vibration on the curb rein. The curb hooks for the chain are on the rings of the upper cheeks of the bit, so anything other than a very short upper cheek pulls the chain above the chin groove on to the branches of the lower jaw (see bottom photo). This will cause the horse discomfort or pain which is likely to cause him to throw his head up rather than doing the opposite and giving to the bit. This problem is made worse by a bit fitted too high in the mouth – an extremely common fault today.

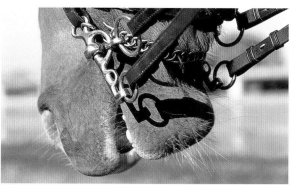

25 Improving your upper body position

The correct, classical, upper body posture is as follows: the upper arms drop downward as they do when hanging naturally with the elbows resting at the hips. The upper body should be held erect, slightly stretched up from the waist, while the seat and legs drop down from the waist. The breastbone should be slightly raised and the shoulders gently pushed back and down.

Elbows too far forward/turned out

Many people ride with their elbows too far forward (see top photo) thinking that they are being kind to their horses by giving with the hands. Unfortunately, other riders ride with their elbows too far forward because, as one put it to me: 'If I hold them where you say, I have nowhere to go when I want to pull back.' As explained elsewhere in this book, pulling back should be avoided.

When the elbows are constantly too far forward, the shoulders tend to droop forward and the chest drops. The sensitivity of the rein contact is lessened and the independence of the hands adversely affected. Moving the hands slightly backwards and forwards to go with the horse's head can be done from the wrists, flexing them slightly backwards and forwards with the head to keep a sensitive, even feel on the horse's mouth. Making this rhythmical back and forth movement with the elbows instead of just the wrists or even fingers can cause rocking of the upper body, creating instability and usually transmitting a slight forward and back movement all the way down to the seat. This will be disturbing and confusing to a classically-schooled horse used to communication from the rider's seatbones and weight. Even horses

ignorant of classical training naturally listen to the rider's weight and, as with the 'white noise' of constantly tapping or kicking legs, they soon switch off from this constant, rocking seat movement and become less and less responsive.

What can I do?

Think of trying to gently touch your hips with your elbows as you ride. Ride for five minutes with a short whip behind your back and held in place in the folds of your arms – this will make you keep your elbows back (albeit too far) and the sheer indignity of it should prevent you from letting your elbows sneak forwards again!

26 Improving the use of the outside rein

The purposes of the outside rein are to help control speed, to assist in turns and pirouettes, to help block the movement of a horse falling out through the outside shoulder or leading with the outside shoulder in leg yield, and to guide the horse into an effective outline or frame within which he can adopt a strong, weight-carrying posture.

When the outside rein is misused

Riders often have an insufficient contact for the horse's stage of training which gives him no instruction at all. The other extreme is to keep the reins too short and tight which restrict the horse's movement and may cause resistances elsewhere in the body, as well as mental upset or bad behaviour. Using the outside rein in a backward movement instead of sideways when making bends, turns and circles can also cause similar faults or even outside flexion.

What can I do?

1 To control speed think of closing or tightening the seat muscles intermittently, and give slightly firmer on-off squeezes with the fingers on the outside rein.
2 To help with bends, turns and circles, press the outside rein sideways on the horse's neck, just in front of the withers, in a gentle but unmistakable press-release technique. Keep your elbow at your hip but give the horse more rein to permit flexion to the inside by giving with or opening the bottom three fingers of your outside hand. Also, lay your outside leg down the horse's side, put your inside seatbone forward a little and,

keeping your inside elbow at your hip, gently feel the inside rein and/or hold it sideways into the turn.
3 To block movement to the outside, press the outside rein sideways on the neck, as above, supporting with the outside leg.
4 To guide the horse in attaining his outline or frame, hold the outside rein gently but firmly, squeeze-and-release on the inside rein to ask him to soften his jaw, and press your inside leg on and off in a slightly forward brushing action immediately behind the girth, directing the energy towards your

outside hand. A horse at the stage of being asked for an outline should understand all these aids and come softly up to the outside hand.

To improve your use of the outside rein and your horse's response to your aids generally, incorporate simple schooling moves into your riding – whether out on a hack or in a manège. Include plenty of turns, bends and circles. With each move ensure you keep your elbow at your hip as you lightly apply the outside rein, using your seat and legs to guide and direct the horse.

27 Knowing how to use an open rein

The use of the rein known as an open rein is extremely useful, and one not always used enough. It is good for guiding or inviting a horse to turn, bend or circle, particularly with a young or green horse, as it seems to be a clearer aid than simply feeling/squeezing the inside rein.

The open rein is applied by simply bringing your inside hand inward towards the centre of your turn, away from your horse. To be more technical, every turn or bend is part of a circle and every circle has a radius leading out from its centre point. Simply carry your hand towards that centre point.

Incorrect use of the open rein

Two common faults of using the open rein are (a) the rider pulls backwards on it, pulling the horse round contrary to classical principles, and (b) the rider's arm moves forwards, losing the contact and much of the effect the rider is trying to achieve.

Pulling the horse around a turn or corner is often accompanied by a backward shift of the inside seatbone, which is exactly opposite to the correct, forward movement recommended. Sometimes, the inside leg even goes forward. The horse will bend his neck but may well 'fall out' through the outside shoulder (the opposite to what you want) unless the rider applies sideways blocking aids with the outside leg and rein. This is an ugly and uncomfortable way to turn.

Putting the arm forwards and in, usually in an attempt to indicate that you want a turn but still with forward impetus, is harmless but fairly useless. The horse may well turn a little but will probably listen more to your seat, leg and outside rein aids.

What can I do?

To open the rein with minimal, or no, disturbance of the upper arm and elbow position, carry your elbows and hands in the correct basic position, thumbs on top, and just turn your inside wrist over so that your fingernails are facing the sky and your thumb is pointing towards the centre of your circle or turn (see left above). You don't have to actually move your forearm sideways, although it will emphasize your request if you do. You will note that with this mere turn of the wrist you have opened your inside rein by the width of your hand, which the horse can feel in his mouth and, because it is a subtle, gentle and calm aid, is guaranteed to obey. I have never known a horse, old or young, which didn't respond.

If you are carrying a whip in your inside hand turning over the wrist will be impossible. In this case, simply *carry* your hand inward towards the centre point of your circle or turn.

28 Improving the use of the inside rein

The inside rein asks the horse to relax his jaw, give to the bit, flex (turn his head) to the inside, turn his whole self that way, stop leaning on the bit, or stop pushing against it which we feel as pulling. It is fine to swing the inside rein a little, vibrate it, squeeze it or give a firmer feel on it according to what is needed to get a result, but pulling is wrong – unless we get into a crisis when all but the most exceptional of us will pull whether we want to or not.

Too much inside rein

The main problem concerning the use of the inside rein is that people tend to pull on it, sometimes straight back, sometimes into a bend or turn and sometimes across the neck or withers. Often it not used with enough tact and subtlety.

If a rider significantly pulls the inside rein, what is likely to happen?

- The horse may resist, pull back and poke his nose
- He may turn his head and neck but not his body (see right)
- He may turn his head and neck but send his body in the opposite direction shoulder first (falling out through the shoulder)
- If the rider is attempting leg yield or shoulder-in and pulls on the inside rein to maintain flexion opposite to the direction of travel, in leg yield the horse will probably fall out through the outside shoulder and simply move straight in a diagonal line to the track (ie not crossing his legs); in shoulder-in, he will probably veer off on a circle away from the track, depending on the rider's other aids

What can I do?

The horse may well be performing these faults because that is how he interpreted the aids he felt – in other words, he did what he thought the rider was asking. Of course, the seat and leg aids can help greatly to correct and prevent them but they would be much less likely to occur if the rider did not actually pull back on the inside rein in the first place.

Assess how much you use the inside rein by asking your horse for leg yield or shoulder-in without holding the inside rein. Simply leave the inside rein loose on the horse's neck and rest your inside hand on your thigh. By applying the correct seat, leg and outside hand aids, your horse should move effortlessly into whichever lateral movement you have asked for. If he carries on around the school and ignores your aids, you will have learnt two things – you use your inside hand more than you thought and your outside aids are not clear enough.

The top right photograph shows a lovely, wide turn with a light, passive inside rein. The bottom left photo shows the horse declining to perform shoulder-in because his rider has too strong an inside rein and has moved her body away (to the right) from the direction in which she wishes to go. In the bottom right photo, she has a much lighter inside rein, and a stronger outside rein to maintain the horse's forehand off the track, and points her outside hip up the track. Because she has got it right, so has he.

29 Correcting your hand position

With your hands in the correct position the thumb should be held on top of the rein, holding it in place against the middle bone of your first or index finger with definite but gentle pressure. In this way, by opening and closing your three lower fingers on each hand, you can give and take a significant amount of rein without having to move the elbow or hand forwards.

Recommending riding with the thumbs on top and the little finger underneath (see bottom photo) may sound like useless fuss, but it does have a purpose. With the hands held in this vertical position, you do have a much more sensitive and direct feel on the rein and horse's mouth and can sense messages from him running up the rein to your hands, as well as deliver them to him with your fingers, mainly your third or ring finger under which the rein will run.

Thumbs not held on top

If you concentrate on holding the rein with the whole of your hand, even though the rein does run under your third finger, you will find that you lose a good deal of subtlety and the potential for variety in giving and receiving aids and messages.

Some riders find their thumbs stick upwards. This indicates tension in the rider. Remember the old saying: Fear runs down the reins. That is true of any emotion – and a sensitive rider can also feel it running up the reins. Other riders find themselves holding the reins in a horizontal position ('pram pushing' or typing). These hands will be much less sensitive and, again, the potential for giving and receiving slight nuances of messages to and from the horse is greatly reduced.

What can I do?

Thinking about holding two wine glasses in your hands with the stems running vertically through them, as described on page 34, will certainly help you keep your thumbs on top.

Try riding with the reins held in a driving style – where the reins run from the horse's mouth, between the thumb and forefinger, down between the palm and fingertips and out below the little finger. The hands are in almost the identical position to correct riding position, but the rein direction changes, running to the hand and down through it. Holding the reins in this way seems not only to almost force you to keep your thumbs on top but also discourages pulling on the reins as you are not used to this hold.

30 Learning to give with one rein

Most of the time the rein with which we give significantly is the inside rein because keeping a contact on the outside rein is fundamental in helping the horse find his way into his outline or frame. However there are times, such as in bends and turns, when the outside fingers open to give a little outside rein to enable or encourage the horse to make his turn while flexing and looking in the direction in which he is turning. In cases where a horse finds it difficult to flex one way, say to the right, it is necessary to keep a contact with the inside (right) rein and give with the outside (left) more than usual, in order to both maintain and allow the flexion to the right.

Inability to use hands independently

Riders who cannot use the reins independently are often insecure in the seat and therefore nervous of letting go. They may subconsciously be using the reins as lifelines. If both reins are used at once in the same way, usually to maintain a firm contact or even a pull, a horse will stiffen the neck and pull back or push forward against the bit (top right). A few horses will come behind the bit in an effort to evade control (bottom right).

What can I do?

It is important to learn to depend more on your seat, legs and mind to direct the horse and to acquire an independent seat which will free the hands to be not only independent of the body but also of each other.

When riding in a school or enclosed area try dropping the inside rein and resting your inside hand on your thigh or the pommel, holding the outside rein as you would when riding normally. Try and move the horse around the school, directing him with your seat and weight. By not holding

the inside rein at all, you cannot be tempted to use it. Change the rein and try it with your other hand only holding the outside rein.

Horses definitely go more kindly when the reins are used tactfully and independently. They seem to feel less constrained and more reassured than by constant pressure on both reins together. While the horse is still learning about achieving and maintaining an outline and self-carriage, it is important that a steady but elastic contact is maintained on the outside rein while the inside is more variable and intermittent.

31 Riding with the correct rein contact

A rider's hands need to guide, encourage, give and take without being harsh or strong. The reins are a means of communication and must not be used to punish or to maintain the rider's balance.

Rider inadvertently stopping the horse

A nervous rider afraid of being run away with at the faster gaits and when jumping can easily become more preoccupied with keeping the horse down to a reasonable speed for control than with developing fluidity and freedom, causing them to pull on the reins subconsciously.

When jumping in particular, many people with this tendency are afraid of falling off and it is this fear that is transmitted to the horse often resulting in the horse refusing. Conversely, a galloping horse will often go faster under a nervous rider because he senses the lack of control, gets nervous himself and does what most frightened horses do if they can – run.

What can I do?

Be realistic about your abilities and genuine fears. Don't struggle on without help or it could result in you or the horse getting injured – which could start you on to the slippery slope towards giving up. Ride more suitable mounts under good instruction until you are more competent and confident. If your own horse is the problem, ride at a slow

pace that you are happy with under instruction from an understanding teacher. Once you have gained confidence, you can progress on to faster gaits.

You need to understand, through a good teacher, exactly what you are doing to stop the horse. You may badly want to do something but are afraid of doing it, such as jumping or cantering or

having a gallop in a wide, open space. You may be pulling back on the reins, clinging on and gripping, or pulling back with your body. The famous 'foetal crouch' is the epitome of fear and the antithesis of a strong, confident seat – and riders often don't realize they are doing it. Try and enjoy your riding – that is why we do it after all!

RELATED AREAS OF IMPROVEMENT · **21** · **27** · **87**

32 Learn to keep your hands still

Keeping your hands still is essential to being able to feel through the reins what is happening in your horse's mouth, in other words what your horse is telling you from this area. If your hands are moving around, this is impossible.

Hands moving up and down

This is another common fault caused by the rider having an insecure, unbalanced seat or the rider not having learned to think of the hands as independent of the body movement. Even some riders with an independent seat cannot do that. This fault is most common in rising trot but can occur in canter.

In trot, as the rider's upper body goes up and down the hands go with it, usually anchoring on the horse's mouth (see above). This is due to a poor rising trot technique in which the rider pushes herself up with her legs and drops down again. In canter, the hands tend to go up and down according to the rider's individual balance. They often go up on the moment of suspension (when the leading leg leaves the ground and the horse's head comes up and back a little) and down as the leading leg lands again (and the head and neck go down and forward). The rider may well feel that she is going with the horse's head movements but it is too exaggerated and disturbs the horse's mouth. This can also be caused, but with a reverse hand action to that described above, because the rider is allowing her upper body to rock backwards and forwards

in canter, a fault which is discussed on page 29.

What can I do?

A much more effective way of performing the rising trot is to do it with the seat instead of the legs. As you rise to the trot, drop and relax your legs down and round the horse rather

than pushing up with them, tilt the lowest part of the pelvis forward rather than up, then allow them to return to 'neutral' as you sit lightly. In this way, you are not performing an up-and-down movement but a forward-and-sit one. With this method the upper body hardly goes up and down at all making it much easier for the rider to keep the hands steady.

33 Maintaining the correct bend during canter transitions

The basic aids for a canter strike-off on a bend are: the outside rein pressed sideways against the neck, just in front of the withers but not crossed over them and with the fingers opened a little. The inside rein is either used as an open rein (see pages 47 and 48) taking care not to pull it backwards, or simply kept in place and squeezed gently with the inside hand raised a little. It is best to give a little with your inside rein at the moment of strike-off to give the horse freedom to do it without fear of a jab in the mouth. Do not lean forward or into the bend. Keeping your upper body upright, put your inside seatbone forward and your outside leg back slightly from the hip, not just the knee, lengthen your inside leg straight down and ask for canter with it in a forward brushing aid. A well-schooled horse will strike into canter just from a forward lift of the inside seatbone.

Incorrect bend during canter strike-off

This riding fault appears in this section of the book because it is often the incorrect use of the rein aids which produce the wrong bend.

If you watch horses cantering and playing at liberty, you'll notice that they sometimes strike off into canter with an outside bend. Horses balance with their heads and necks and, when turning on a short, tight turn, particularly at speed, they do put the head to the outside of the turn to counterbalance their heavy bodies. As a prey animal, a horse's eyes are placed well to the sides of his head, so he doesn't actually need to turn his head to see where he is going because he can see almost all around him anyway – with his head flexed to the right on a left curve, he can easily see where he is going well to the left. So why do we ask that he looks into his turns and circles in the direction to which he is going? Being vertical and

not horizontal animals and with a predator eye set on the front of the skull looking forwards, we think that it is more logical to do this and so, illogically, we school our very differently-made horses to do it, too.

What can I do?

To encourage inside bend during canter strike-offs, always ask for the transition in a corner of the manège or as part of a circle. By doing this, the horse will already be following the shape of the circle and looking to the inside. Open the inside rein a little to encourage the inside bend if necessary. To improve the rider's effectiveness of the aids during canter strike-offs, try working on the lunge. The rider can then concentrate purely on the aids as the horse will already have the correct bend established.

As with all training, we aim to build up a horse's muscles and body strength so that he can perform as we see fit and carrying our weight. With a young, green or unfit horse, it is often wise to allow him strike off into canter with the wrong bend in the early stages of his training because he has enough to cope with just getting into canter with weight on his back. As he builds up strength and expertise, we can gradually ask for a straight head and neck position and finally for a flexion into the curve.

Head

Use your head

We tend to think of weight, seat, hands, legs and so on, but what effect can the head have on influencing how a horse goes? In practice, it can have a great effect, especially on the mind which we always think of as being in the head because it seems to be interwoven with the brain. I won't get into too much of a discussion about that but, as anyone living in the modern world can't fail to have noticed, there is a good deal of emphasis on the body/mind/spirit approach to life these days.

On a physical level

Remember that our heads are heavy and even a shift in head posture, angle or direction will be sensed by the horse. This seems amazing, particularly as such a change may be so slight as to seem insignificant to the onlooker. In fact, many highly-schooled horses will alter their actions just because they sense a change, voluntary or involuntary, in their rider's head position – provided the rider is not blocking the horse in some other way, purposely or otherwise. It's an extremely subtle interaction.

From a balance and control point of view it is best to keep the head central above the spine and to maintain the classical ear-shoulder-elbow/hip-ankle bone vertical line when viewed from the side. When viewed from the front or back, the shoulders and hips should be level with the head held straight exactly above the spine. Try to keep your face directed between your horse's ears whichever way he is flexed and just move your eyes (see pages 64 and 65) to look in the direction in which you wish to go.

On a mental level

Try these exercises next time you ride to prove just how influential your mind is on your riding and your horse.

1 Ask someone to walk beside your horse, just in case, have a loose rein, loosen the muscles of your seat and legs and close your eyes. Take your time and try to feel where your awareness or mind is. Next open your eyes and try again to feel where it is.

   Most people find that in the eyes-closed mode their awareness is in the seat area or centre, where we want it to be, but with the eyes open it is in the head. They often add that in the first mode they feel much more tuned in to their horse which is exactly what we want. In the second mode they start to feel top-heavy. This demonstrates how important it is to control our mind/awareness and to direct it down to our centre – even with our eyes open. This also has the effect of 'lightening' the head.

2 Ask your horse to make a turn with just your mind and eyes. Make a clear decision about which way you want to turn and think to the horse which way you want to go, without doing anything at all with your body. A passive body can be quite tricky to achieve at first but most riders get it after a few minutes. Direct the horse with your mind only and visualize the pair of you turning in the required direction. Provided a rider maintains a passive body – the horse usually turns in the correct direction, maybe a little uncertainly at first, then with more confidence – and the more times it is repeated in a session, the more definite the horse becomes.

So don't underestimate the effect of your head on your horse. Riding with the spirit as well as with the body and mind is the ideal way to obtain results, as well as developing a partnership with your horse.

34 Ensuring you look ahead when riding

Looking up and ahead while riding may sound obvious, but by keeping the head directly above the shoulders, a rider maintains their balance, it strengthens the upper body and helps maintains good posture – as well as letting them see where they are going! If looking down is your fault, you are in the best company in the world because it was the admitted fault of none other than Portuguese maestro, the late Nuño Oliveira, probably the best and most revered classical horseman of the 20th century. You can see it in most of his photos and he used to joke about it, saying that everyone is entitled to one fault and that was his.

Looking down

Looking down physically alters your balance slightly and many people who look down tend to lean forward (although Nuño Oliveira didn't) and think downwards with the shoulders and body. This can weaken the seat and lessen upper body posture and control. If your head is tipped downwards you tend not to look around and become less aware of your immediate surroundings. It denies you the benefit of 'soft eyes', as Sally Swift teaches in her classic books on centred riding. Having 'soft eyes' means that you are aware of things in your peripheral area of vision slightly out of focus. Also, have you ever had that unsettling feeling that someone behind you is staring at you? Looking down at the back of your horse's head mentally pressurizes him.

What can I do?

The simple way to overcome this problem is to just keep telling yourself (along with all the other things you have to nag yourself about) to 'look ahead'. Looking down instead of ahead also makes it difficult to keep your awareness in your centre/seat area. Try it and see.

Another tactic is to give yourself a high marker ahead of you to look at and ride towards. This focuses your attention upwards on to something specific. Keep looking at it and, as you reach it or change direction, say in turns and circles, find another marker quickly and ride towards that. Riding circles in the shape of an octagon, with several little

straight lines instead of a continuous curve can help some people to use the above technique as you have to find several markers to look at and progress from one to the next. (Because of the frequent need to bring the forehand in front of the hindquarters at the end of each short line, it also helps to gets the weight back on to the hindquarters.)

35 Improving your head posture

Remember the classical position guideline of keeping your ears above your shoulders on a straight, vertical line. Apart from being unsightly, a head pushed out of alignment can cause poor distribution of weight and energy because it adversely influences the posture of the neck, shoulders and upper body. The amount of feel you get from your horse will be lessened as will the sensitivity of your hands in giving aids and listening to your horse.

Head pushed forward or back

The most common fault of the two is having the head pushed forwards, probably because it is the easiest. Needless to say, if the head is pushed forwards, it may well also be tipped downwards making it impossible to maintain the erect, upright body posture which is so essential to good flatwork. The shoulders are the first to follow this faulty head position, then the chest drops and, if things go even further, the rider may collapse at the waist and slouch in the saddle, coming off the seatbones and necessitating a complete re-jig of his or her position.

When the head is pushed backwards, the rider normally experiences stiffness down the back of the neck and across the upper shoulders which almost always affects the rider's arms and, ultimately, hands.

What can I do?

Tension and over-concern to ride well are the most common causes for a head to be pushed forwards or back, although they can certainly be exacerbated by physical problems in the rider. General body control exercises and relaxation techniques can help although physical problems need to be identified and treated by a medical professional first.

Here is an extremely simple exercise that can be carried out both in and out of the saddle. Gently circle your head on its joint with the top of the spine. Circle first one way, then the other. Gently push it towards its limits of movement so that you feel the tissues in your neck and shoulders being slightly stretched. These exercises are excellent for many head and shoulder posture and stiffness problems but readers new to bodywork of this sort should take expert advice from an appropriate practitioner first.

36 Improving your peripheral vision

It is quite possible to look where you're going without focusing directly on where you want to go by developing your proprioception skills – your awareness of your body and its surroundings. You may read this thinking: 'But my instructor is always telling me to look where I'm going!' Yes, but not to the exclusion of being aware of your surroundings and of giving your horse and yourself a bit of leeway in your movements.

Tunnel vision

This is a fault shown by many riders who look and think doggedly ahead and take no notice of what's happening in their immediate environment, even to the point of colliding with jumps, instructors and other riders!

What can I do?

One way to lessen the tendency to stare straight ahead is to aim for dressage markers, landmarks and directions without looking straight at them but holding them in your peripheral vision and practise arriving there using more feel than sight. This involves developing your proprioception skills – your awareness of where various parts of your body are or, in this case, your whole body. Practise looking ahead but absorbing what's nearby by getting a friend or your instructor to hold up various objects as you ride past. Without looking at her, call out what the objects are. It sounds silly but it does help and it does work.

When it comes to jumping, many riders look at the jumps themselves, which can actually stop a horse. It can really help you get over a jump or combination via your selected track if you have some marker at the far side of your fences to keep your eyes on and aim for. This technique makes you ride much more by feel and actually takes your attention off the fences which are preoccupying you. When jumping a course, get into the habit of looking to your next fence well in advance of approaching it.

RELATED AREAS OF IMPROVEMENT   34   94   95

37 Removing tension from your upper body

Tension in the upper body is quite common and is often shown in a tilted head position. Mental tension in general usually comes out somewhere in the body, the upper body and particularly the head and shoulders are common sites for it. This usually causes stiffness or inco-ordination in the hands and arms, leading to a blockage of energy and poor and harsh communication, so learning to overcome it is important.

Head tilting to one side

Head tilting is a common fault in riders who pressurize themselves. Often when the head tilts to one side the shoulder on that side rises a little too, causing stiffness in the arm, maybe even with a sideways raising of the elbow and reduced sensitivity and efficiency in the hand. Sometimes the hand becomes so affected and prone to stiffness that it causes resistance problems in the horse's mouth. There is always a knock-on effect with physical stiffness, even where there is no pain involved. Sometimes, the horse may start cutting corners or falling in on the side to which the head is tilted because the rider is putting extra weight, even if only a little, on the seatbone on that side, and horses tend to go where you put your weight.

What can I do?

The easiest way to tell if you are tilting your head to one side is to have someone on the ground telling you when you are doing it (and it is almost always to the same side every time). If you are on your own, another way of telling if you are tilting your head is to look up at the peak or brim of your riding hat. If the hat is on straight and your head is straight, the peak or brim will be straight in relation to the surrounding landscape. If your head is crooked, your hat peak or brim will be slanted down towards the side to which your head is tilted.

Simple exercises for the head and neck will help to gently stretch the soft tissues of the neck and upper shoulders making this area more supple. See page 59. Rolling the shoulders backwards and forwards, does a similar job. Lift up your shoulders as high as you can, as though trying to touch your ears with them, then push the shoulders back and down.

38 Keeping your head still

Regard your body as being in two halves: the upper body belongs to you, the lower body belongs to your horse. You have to stretch up from the waist and drop down from the waist. Imagine the waist itself as being made of jelly or foam rubber – it is here and in the small of your back that the force or energy is absorbed and dissipated, never reaching the upper body.

Concentrate on holding your upper body up and very slightly back from the horse's head and neck and on dropping (not pushing) your seat and weight loosely down, in the classical seat described on pages 6 and 7. You first need to develop the technique (ideally on the lunge) of keeping your seat and leg muscles completely loose – then you are in a position to absorb the energy coming up from the horse.

The chief mechanism in your back for absorbing the movement of the sitting trot is the lumbo-sacral joint in your lower spine, between the lumbar or lower back/loin area and the sacrum below it, a virtually solid bone structure consisting of five fused vertebrae at the bottom or small of your back. The flexing of the lumbo-sacral joint, forwards and backwards, is what enables you to absorb the horse's movement beneath your seat.

Nodding head

Riders with nodding heads in sitting trot are commonly seen and this occurs purely because the rider is not correctly absorbing the movement of the horse through the lower back. The energy is travelling right up the spine, coming out at the top.

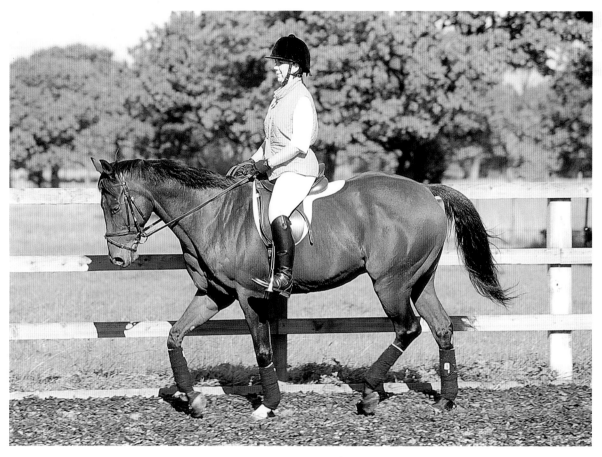

What can I do?

Establish a balanced working trot sitting, then steady it down a little. As the horse rises and pushes you up in the suspension phase of trot, accept the force up into your seat by slightly rounding or flattening the small of your back. This gives you the feeling of bringing your seatbones up and forward with the horse's back as it rises. As the horse lands, slightly hollow the small of your back to absorb the impact softly in your seat as you feel it going down with his back.

What is actually happening is that your lumbo-sacral joint is opening towards your horse's tail as you round the small of your back and closing again as you hollow it. Your pelvis is attached by very short, strong ligaments to each side of your sacrum at two joints called the sacro-iliac joints. Therefore, as you flatten and hollow the small of your back the pelvis has to tilt with it.

To help you feel stuck to the

saddle, so that you have to go with the movement of the horse, imagine that you have glue all over the underside of your breeches or jodhpurs giving you a flexible but secure bond with your saddle.

39 Directing your horse with the eyes

I have already discussed directing your horse with your mind, (pages 56 and 57). Now I'd like to describe another technique, which, because it can exert no physical influence whatsoever on the horse, can also be described as a mind technique – that of turning the horse with only your eyes.

Basically – look where you want to go, not where you don't want to go. When you want to make a turn just turn your eyes in the direction you have chosen, being very certain that you do not indicate with any other part of your body which way you want to go – just turn your eyes. The horse will usually comply and turn in the direction in which you are looking.

It's easy to give out the wrong signals

The following scenario is a good example of how a horse can misread the signals from a rider:

A rider is riding along the track aiming to perform a shoulder-in. The horse is going with good, calm, forward impulsion and kindly accepting the bit in a good outline with his nose just in front of the vertical. They arrive at a corner of the school and ride a circle, the rider's classical aids for a turn are: inside seatbone forward, inside hand raised a little and inviting the horse into the turn, outside leg back slightly to support the turn and remind the hindquarters not to swing out and the outside rein pressed lightly against the neck just in front of the withers. The rider's face is directed between the horse's ears, eyes looking around the circle.

Returning to the corner, the rider requests shoulder-in by continuing around the circle until the horse's forefeet are off the track. The rider then moves the outside seatbone and leg forward, presses sideways with a lengthened inside leg, brings the inside rein to touch the neck just in front of the withers keeping the mouth contact very light and, depending on the individual horse, either invites him up the track with the outside rein or keeps it in touch near the withers to keep the forehand off the track. The rider's face is still directed between the horse's ears – but so are the eyes. What happens? The horse shows a little confusion but continues resolutely round the circle, not up the track in shoulder-in. The rider tries again with the same result, then remembers to look where they want to go. Asking again, the rider looks up the track – and this time the horse performs a beautiful shoulder-in. I have seen this happen so many times.

I was once teaching a horse and rider in a jumping lesson – they were on a right-hand track, jumping well, when someone outside the manège called to the rider from the left. The rider instinctively looked slightly left, the horse whipped left and they crashed into a nearby jump.

These are only two examples of just how effective an aid your eyes are, to both good and bad effect.

What can I do?

Practise directing your horse with your eyes by riding in a relaxed walk, on a long and ideally a loose rein so that the horse will regard this as a sign to relax – no orders, no effort, no brain work – simply chill out. When you are both quite calm, sit still and loose (no aids at all), keep your face directed between your horse's ears and try to keep your mind out of gear. Now just turn your eyes in the direction you have chosen. Be very certain that you do not indicate with any other part of your body which way you want to go – just turn your eyes.

The horse will comply and turn in the direction in which you are looking, maybe a little uncertainly at first. If he even suggests taking part of a step in the correct direction, praise him immediately. Try again and this time he will be more definite. Next try for the opposite direction – then try serpentines, loops, circles, even a figure of eight.

Shoulders and back

Sitting pretty

Riding is a matter for the whole body and mind and, although the expression 'the seat' is still used to describe how a rider sits on a horse, uses the body and applies the aids, one of the most obvious qualities of this deportment is how the rider is seen to carry the upper body. If you look at almost any Spanish or Portuguese classical rider you will notice a held but supple, erect posture which suggests pride and elegance. This posture is described and recommended several times throughout this book, including on pages 6 and 7, and its importance cannot be over-emphasized.

Working in harmony

Some methods of equitation seem to regard it as a virtue to almost crouch and to swing the upper body ('going with the horse') when riding as if this posture were generous to the horse. I have tried several other systems of riding but have always come back to classicism because it works in harmony with the horse and is safer than any other method I have tried.

The classical position, both for flatwork and jumping, is safer precisely because of the posture taught to students by good instructors. It teaches them to be physically independent, yet still able to blend with the horse's movements. When looking at a mounted rider you should be able to imagine a straight, vertical line dropped from the ear, through the shoulder, through the elbow and hip (the elbow being held at the hip) and through the ankle bone to the ground. From the back, the shoulders and hips should be level. This basic upper body position is excellent, but there are a few refinements which make it perfect.

The head should be held up – it may help to gently press the back of your neck into your collar. The shoulders should be gently pushed back and down, with the breastbone raised a little. Some teachers recommend expanding the ribcage. Do not hollow your back in response to raising your chest – an extremely common reaction, which will give you backache in no time. It is better to do one of the following three things which, in practice, are all more or less the same and result in a controlled, balanced and comfortable posture in the saddle: tuck your bottom under slightly, push your hip joints forward a little and allow the small of your back to flatten a little.

Hold the muscles of your upper body in slight tension or tone to keep it independent of the horse's movement, ensuring you do not slop around or allow the horse to pull you about. This is by no means stiffness or rigidity, but muscle tone and control – a skill you will develop with practice. It is also important to be able to hold your elbows back at your hips by the same technique. If someone pushes your elbow from behind, you should be able to keep it in place by means of muscular tone and resistance, not by pushing against them.

The upper body posture and 'hold' plus the deep, independent seat of the lower body are what enable the rider to balance and control themselves, to stay on the horse in most circumstances, to sit passively but in control when required, to accompany the horse's movements when appropriate and to actively influence the horse when needed. Without body discipline a rider cannot do these things. Never force your position as this creates mental and physical tension, inhibits effective use of the aids and is transmitted to your horse.

Certain non-riding techniques can help you understand and achieve body discipline, strength and control. These include dancing (particularly ballet and ballroom dancing), gymnastics, skating, yoga, Pilates, Feldenkrais and the Alexander Technique.

40 Improving your upper body posture

The upper body is the rider's autonomy when riding. Apart from maintaining your balance with a toned and held upper body, you can use and control your lower body (seat, weight and legs) much more effectively and so guide and control your horse to a better extent.

Shoulders rolled forwards

If you don't keep your shoulders back and down, sit up and raise your breastbone somewhat, you will find maintaining your balance with an independent upper body difficult.

People who ride and walk with their shoulders forward may be naturally round-shouldered or may have a spinal conformation which enforces this. However, as long as they can hold their upper bodies as erect as they can within their own capabilities, this shouldn't adversely affect their riding.

What can I do?

To loosen up your shoulders circle them backwards several times a day, particularly if you have been sat in one position, say over a desk, for a while. You can also do these exercises while you ride your horse. As you give your horse a chance to rest and relax during a schooling session, take a moment to run through your own position and correct as necessary. When you are not riding try and get into the habit of sitting or standing more upright in the way described on pages 62 and 63.

Another useful exercise for stretching the shoulder muscles is to draw large backward circles with the arm. Take the arm out in front of you, keep looking forwards, draw the arm up and past your ear, back and down. Repeat with the other arm. Remember, particularly with the latter exercise, not to force any movement but to take it to the limits of what you feel is comfortable with a slight push. You could also consider starting bodywork practices such as dancing, Pilates, yoga, Alexander Technique and Feldenkrais or even just general fitness and suppleness classes or exercises. Swimming backstroke can also help. With any such regime, it may be best to consult your doctor or a physiotherapist before you start, especially if you are not used to exercise or if you have any conformational problem or injury, past or present.

41 Removing tension from your shoulders

Tension is considered a fault in riding because it adversely affects the whole of the rider's body communication with the horse. Any tension blocks the passage of energy and causes tenseness in other areas of the body. Even mental communication is affected by physical tension. This is proved time and again – once riders become more calm and relaxed in body and mind, they find that their horses respond better and more quickly to their thoughts and physical aids. How many times have we seen horses, particularly highly-strung, very sensitive types, improve vastly under a more relaxed rider, even if he or she is not so technically competent as a previous rider?

Hunched shoulders

Tight, hunched shoulders are nearly always a sign of tension in the rider – perhaps from fear of riding, a fear of the particular horse they are on, they are trying too hard or are anxious about not being able to ride well or about looking foolish in front of the teacher or onlookers. It may, of course, also be shown by people who are generally tense about life in general.

What can I do?

If you are tense you may benefit from learning a relaxation technique. Learn to meditate, use aromatherapy oils (lavender, for instance) around the home and in your bath, or indulge in a professional aromatherapy massage now and then. Give yourself a break and designate daily periods when you can switch off your mind and listen to soporific music. Anything which helps you to calm down and relax is well worth it.

To help relax your shoulders, sit or stand upright without hollowing your back, gently press your shoulders

back and down and raise your chest or breastbone a little. Try it in front of a large mirror and see what a difference it can make. Familiarize yourself with the feeling of being in the correct posture, then try it in the saddle. Circle your shoulders

backwards and forwards several times, then try the same exercise with your arms. This will help stretch the soft tissues in the area and increase the joints' mobility.

42 Strengthening your overall position

Self-carriage and body control apply to riders as well as horses. Riders must acquire the knack of holding the upper body above the waist up and independent of what is going on underneath them. This is achieved by keeping the muscles of the torso above the waist lightly tensed or 'toned' without stiffness or rigidity. Otherwise, the horse can disturb the rider's balance and autonomy with his own movements to the detriment of control and performance.

Collapsed waist

Sometimes riders collapse at the waist because they are trying too hard to get the horse to go in a particular direction, usually away from the side to which they have collapsed. For example, in trying to leg yield to the left, the rider may collapse to the right by trying to put the outside (left) seatbone forward to direct the horse or lengthen the inside (right) leg.

Another occasion when a rider may collapse to the inside is on a bend or circle. It is often seen in sitting trot or canter as the rider makes an effort to follow the horse. Or the rider may collapse forwards, or lean forwards from the waist, when trying hard, but incorrectly, to obtain a transition to canter.

When collapsing at the waist, riders often let their upper body posture go – the shoulders come forward, the chest sinks and the whole effectiveness of their balance and seat is lessened. Some novice riders may also find themselves so preoccupied with other things, not least the way the horse is going or what their teacher is saying, that they simply forget to do what is not yet second nature to them – to hold themselves erect and in balance.

What can I do?

Learning correct upper body posture and keeping it through mental nagging, and acquiring supple but definite upper body tone and strength are how to avoid this quite common fault. In addition to riding, dismounted exercise is a great help (especially as you get older!) to achieve and maintain the strength of the back and abdomen. Some of the modalities already mentioned such as Pilates and yoga are helpful, or consider a carefully graduated whole-body fitness programme, putting the emphasis on developing core body strength and control.

43 Learning to sit erect but relaxed

The human spine has a natural, gentle S-shape and the lower forward curve occurs at the small of the back or loins where the spine curves towards the tummy. If you refer to pages 6 and 7 where the classical seat is discussed, you will find references to the different positions of the pelvis, seatbones and spine which involve slight arching or flattening of this lower forward curve. The normal position of the spine is in 'neutral', neither particularly flattened nor arched beyond the spine's natural shape. This enables the rider who has learned to relax the seat and thigh muscles to sit lightly on the seatbones.

Back too arched

Riders who constantly ride with a back that is too arched must not only suffer terrible backache, but must also be sitting on their forks, putting them out of the desired vertical, straight-line position. Sitting in this way means they cannot use their seat effectively and will ride with their legs too far forward. It is very difficult to ride with the legs in the correct position and be able to move them forwards and back to give leg aids when the bottom is tilted back, the spine is too arched and the rider is on her fork. For anatomical reasons, men don't often exhibit this fault!

What can I do?

dismounted – try stretching up as if you are trying to touch the sky with the top of your head then, staying erect, push your hip joints (where your legs join your torso) slightly forward, tucking your bottom very slightly under at the same time. Aim to get your shoulder blades a fraction behind your hips. Relax and repeat.

mounted – try riding, just in walk, without your stirrups – keep your upper body erect and let your legs hang limply down, without trying to bring your toes up (this will stiffen the lower leg). Slightly push your seatbones/hip joints forward and let the small of your back flatten a little. This will help you to get the feel of a pelvis in a neutral position.

Shoulders and back

44 Assessing your upper body straightness

Straightness is needed in the rider just as much as in the horse, as lack of it inevitably means faulty distribution of weight which sends all the wrong signals to the horse. Horses nearly always go where the rider's weight is, so if the rider inadvertently rides crookedly, she will never get the results she wants or expects.

Twisted spine

Riding with the spine twisted can be yet another manifestation of anxiety and/or poor balance. It is often seen that people under a lot of stress, who are, or have been, ill or those with nagging physical problems often lose previously good posture and control. From the point of view of a rider, anxiety, however it comes out, is usually caused by concern about the horse's performance or behaviour, trying too hard to improve their riding, or trying to do well in public or during a lesson.

Walking or riding with a twisted spine can arise from an old back or leg injury for which the person has compensated by twisting or leaning slightly to one side to avoid the discomfort or pain of standing and moving properly. Long after the pain has gone there may remain a slight shortening of the muscles and associated soft tissues, which may pull the spine slightly out of alignment or cause the person to lean or twist because it is more comfortable to do that than to correct the posture.

What can I do?

If a twisted spine is evident on the ground as well as in the saddle, it would seem a good plan to consult a specialist such as your doctor, a physiotherapist, a chiropractor, an osteopath or other physical therapist. If the problem only arises when riding, there is a chance that the saddle could be unbalanced, or that the horse himself has significantly uneven muscle development, conformation or action. A good saddler can amend the saddle, but if the horse himself is the cause, it may be he who needs a physical therapist of some kind.

If you find you are riding with a twisted spine through anxiety, a lack of balance or just through habit, have a session on the lunge and work on stretching and loosening the muscles of your back. Great exercises include twisting at the waist with your arms stretched out from your sides, or pretending to move your hands up an imaginary rope in front of you to stretch your upper body up and straighten your spine.

45 Improving your balance

In order to ride in control, balance and safety a rider needs to have acquired a deep, secure and independent seat and an upper body which has an erect back, shoulders positioned back and down and a raised chest. This posture is held in place by muscular tone or slight tension. Until this is achieved, the rider can be easily moved around by the horse, unbalanced and dislodged.

Leaning forward

We hear so much from instructors and read so much in books about how important it is to get our horses to go forward, forward, forward that we, not unreasonably, think that by leaning forward ourselves – often pushing our hands forward and dropping the contact into the bargain – it will encourage the horse to do so. It doesn't. All it does is weaken the rider's seat, dilute his or her balance and so lessen communication and control. Leaning forward is certainly instinctive instead of logical. Think of the foetal crouch to which we all resort when we're scared stiff. However, this riding attitude not only frightens or at least hypes up many horses, it also puts the rider in a weak and vulnerable situation.

Of course, there are times when leaning forward is helpful and correct, namely when riding at fast gaits, over obstacles or uphill.

What can I do?

The only way you can check whether or not you are leaning forward, is by using a mirror fixed to one side of a school or by getting someone knowledgeable on the ground to tell you.

As you ride, think of actually leaning back, with your shoulders pushed back and down. You should soon feel more balanced which will then make it feel more natural. Look up and around as you ride pushing your neck back into your collar – remember your head is heavy, if it tips forward it is likely to pull the rest of you forward.

46 Improving your transition position

To send the horse forward or to make a transition, the rider should simply tilt or push the lower pelvis/seatbones forward while the upper body remains upright and balanced – stopping as soon as the horse complies. If this is insufficient, the inside leg can be used in a forward, brushing movement from just behind the girth.

Leaning back

In the UK, at least, many riders appear to be taught a faulty seat, leaning back from the waist in what they seem to regard as a 'driving seat' which is sometimes accompanied by a nodding head (see pages 62 and 63). Apart from being ugly (see above), this is incorrect as it puts the rider in the wrong balance and out of the straight shoulder-hip-ankle posture. Leaning back sometimes occurs when a rider over-compensates for leaning forward, usually when riding without supervision. And when a rider leans too far back other faults may start to creep in, such as sitting on the buttocks instead

of the seatbones, a rounded back (slouching) and the legs positioned too far forward. Leaning back adversely affects the rider's balance and effectiveness, but in combination with other faults, the rider is left in a very weak position.

What can I do?

One of the best ways to improve your position is to have some lunge lessons on a steady horse. This will allow you to concentrate purely on what your instructor is telling you and your position without having to worry about controlling the horse.

47 Improving your shoulder alignment

For a helpful, independent upper body position, the rider should hold the back upright with the shoulders pressed gently but definitely back and down and almost always level with each other. The shoulders are used in vertical alignment with the hips when performing turns and lateral movements. If the shoulders are not held evenly the position of the spine is adversely affected.

Dropping a shoulder

If a rider drops one shoulder it is usually towards the direction in which the rider wishes to go, and, is a lesser version of collapsing at the waist or leaning in. It can also be a sign of tension. A rider may do it to compensate for poor balance, but it can itself put the body out of balance if it is done for some other reason. Of course, it can also be due to stiffness or pain in the rider from an old or current injury.

What can I do?

If the cause of dropping a shoulder is stiffness or pain elsewhere in your body, then this will have to be treated before you can expect much improvement. You could start with a basic aromatherapy massage from a qualified practitioner for a general toning and loosening up, especially if you are not particularly aware of any problem in yourself.

If it is just a bad habit, think of having tumblers of water on your shoulders which you have to keep steady and level. Ask someone on the ground, your teacher or a knowledgeable friend, to observe you critically from front and back in all gaits, and tell you honestly whether or not your shoulders, and the rest of you, are in the correct position.

If tension and an over-anxiety to do well are the causing factors, calming down and not trying too hard is obviously the key to curing your problems. Try relaxation techniques, meditation, aromatherapy or music – whatever helps to switch off your mind. Other areas of your life may benefit from this too. Think about setting your sights a little lower – be happy with what you achieve in your lessons and remember – you ride for enjoyment, not persecution.

Compensating for poor balance can be corrected by working on your seat while on the lunge. Sit with the seat completely opened, loose and relaxed across the horse's back with your legs dangling absolutely loose. I find this the best way to learn to ride entirely by balance because you have nothing else to keep you on.

Incorporate stretching exercises into your lunge session to help improve your overall suppleness – arm and shoulder circles are particularly good for riders who tend to drop a shoulder.

48 Improving balance in canter transitions

Your upper body posture is important for your balance: with poor posture it is difficult to achieve good canter transitions. When asking for canter, sit upright, not forward, warn the horse whilst in sitting trot of your wish to canter by putting your inside seat bone and shoulder forward, your outside leg back slightly and ask with the inside leg. Saying 'canter' will also help.

Collapsing in canter strike-off

Collapsing forwards during canter transitions is almost always caused by one of two things – anxiety to get the canter strike-off or poor balance through a lack of an independent seat and torso.

What can I do?

If you know your horse will canter but are still anxious, include plenty of canter transitions into your schooling sessions so that you build up your trust, confidence and belief in him. Think about incorporating canter transitions into your hacking, if you have suitable riding terrain – you and your horse are likely to be more relaxed, allowing the transitions to happen more naturally.

Remember – tipping forward as you ask for a canter transition is much more likely to keep a horse in trot than to encourage him to canter. If your problem is more of a genuine collapse than a forward lean, you need to improve your upper body strength and control. A dismounted exercise regime aimed at improving back and abdominal strength will greatly help.

As with many problems, a big help with this one is to remind yourself about the upright torso position and be firm with yourself in keeping it as you approach your transition, ask and go.

Looking down encourages people to tip forward, so look ahead and just nag yourself to stay upright – slightly tense those back muscles and aim to keep away from your horse's head and neck. Think of keeping your shoulders fractionally behind your hips as your horse strikes off.

Put your horse where you want to go

Many years ago I watched a television interview with a Battle of Britain pilot on television. One expression he used has stayed with me ever since and I have found it a mental master key when describing 'attitude' to riders who are rather reticent or uncertain.

The pilot was talking about the handling qualities of a Spitfire he had flown during the war and said: 'All you had to do was strap one of those to your backside and you could go anywhere.'

Note: 'you could go anywhere', not 'it would take you anywhere' – a subtle but vast difference in viewpoint. His attitude to the plane was clear – it was he who was going places – the plane was a willing and co-operative tool which enabled him to go where he wanted and do what he wanted, or do what he had to in his case. Obviously he never even thought about his attitude because there was never any chance that the plane wouldn't do as he told it. A plane is clearly a machine which does as it's told, but a horse isn't.

Elsewhere in this book I have said that you need to be calm, firm and positive with horses. If you can cultivate the viewpoint that you are strapping your horse to your backside as a tool to enable you to go where you want to, never even dreaming that he won't go, you will acquire a much more inherently positive attitude to your riding. Horses generally respond favourably to calm, firm, positive people – and so do other people. Next time you get on your horse, don't let him take you for a ride. Aim for a particular marker, gateway, tree or whatever with your seat, your eyes and your expectation and, as you ride for it, mentally put the horse there in front of your legs.

Remember: You are the pilot. Strap your horse to your backside and put him where you want to go – calmly, firmly and positively.

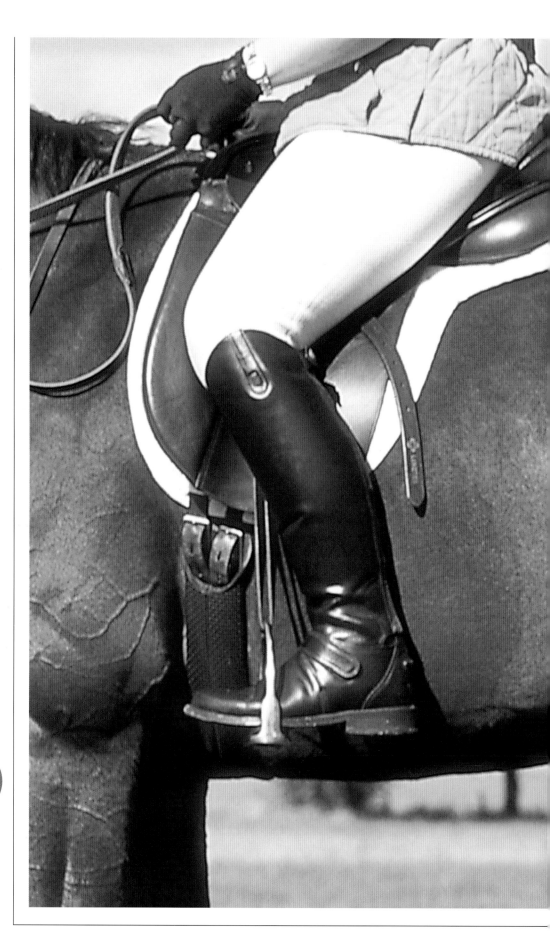

Legs

The long and short of it

My first riding master used to tell beginners: 'The idea is that you keep a leg on each side of the pony and you don't dismount without permission' – in other words, don't fall off. Sound advice.

Each of your legs comprises about 25 per cent of your bodyweight. Legs are very strong, muscular parts of your body and it is almost irresistibly tempting to use them. The trick is in learning to use them only when needed, at other times letting them rest down and around the horse.

Toned but relaxed

It is perfectly possible to hold your legs in gentle muscular tone and readiness, close to your horse's sides but not actually pressing or rubbing significantly – certainly not to the extent that you rub two bare patches on your horse's sides.

When on a horse, we tend to forget that our legs extend downwards from our hips, not our knees. The thighs are dual purpose in riding insomuch as they are part of the seat and part of the legs. The seat should be regarded as everything that comes into contact with the saddle, so it is not only made up of the fork and buttocks, but the insides of the thighs as well. I find that this way of thinking about the seat helps riders trying to grasp the concept of riding with the seat. Giving an aid with the whole leg, such as when asking for a lateral movement or a turn away from a particular leg, is so much more effective than merely using the lower leg.

Using the leg correctly

A remark I often hear is that riders do not actually know how to use the leg. Do you kick, squeeze, grip, jiggle, pinch, tap or brush the horse's sides? It does depend on the type of horse you have and his level of schooling. Some are more responsive than others and will respond to a light brush, others need a tap or even a firm pinch. Jiggling (very common), gripping (again, common but not as an aid) and a sustained squeeze (which deadens the horse's sides) seem to be natural to humans, but do not elicit a crisp response from horses.

Generally, to ask the horse to go forward (if he has ignored your seat/voice aid), try giving the leg aid from immediately behind the girth where he is most sensitive, in a forward, brushing movement. If this, too, is ignored, a firm inward, (not backward) pinch in the same place should work, using both legs if necessary.

49 Developing a deeper seat

You cannot develop a deep seat if your seat muscles are tensed and tight. It is also difficult if you find it hard to open your hips sideways. Loose muscles are also needed in the legs to enable them to drop down around the horse. With these three attributes you will find that balancing and staying on become so much easier and your horse will go much better.

Gripping up with the legs

The reason riders grip up with their legs is entirely through insecurity, although sometimes it appears to be subconscious. As well as gripping with the legs, the rider is often seen hanging on by the reins. A reasonably experienced rider can disguise these faults by simply developing a 'hard' position and seat showing stiffness and lack of feel, and riding with a constantly pulling, hard contact on the reins.

As a nervous rider's legs grip up, the upper body position often begins to slump forwards, or into the foetal crouch. This can be accompanied by hands flailing about, knees up, heels up and toes down as the rider desperately

hangs on. The seat then slides to the back of the saddle and the rider's balance and control become non-existent. Even when the fault is fairly slight and the rider simply has trouble relaxing throughout the body and dropping the legs, other problems are not far away. He or she cannot develop a deep, independent seat thus reducing the potential for good balance, while the hands may jab at the horse's mouth in a play for stability.

The effect on the horse depends on the horse himself – some take gripping legs as an aid to shoot off, often unseating the rider in the process, some react violently to the jabbing, harsh contact on the bit and yet others stoically put up with everything.

What can I do?

The cure for this, as for many faults, is to go back to lunge lessons without reins or stirrups on a steady, reliable horse with smooth gaits. Return to basics and practise letting the muscles of the seat and legs completely relax and find your natural balance.

on the lunge Hold the pommel of the saddle (with the inside hand to counteract centrifugal force at faster gaits) and ensure you are sitting on your seatbones. Hold your upper body in the classical posture and find your natural balance. As you feel more secure, gradually let go of the pommel. Progress until you can ride at walk, trot and canter without the need to grip.

off the lunge Incorporate plenty of work without stirrups into your flatwork and lessons to ensure your legs hang naturally without tension. If you feel your legs starting to grip, carry out simple leg exercises such as lifting one leg away from the saddle, then the other, or swinging the legs forwards and back from the hips.

How long are your legs?

You may encounter problems in keeping your lower leg in the correct position if your horse is simply too big or too small for you. Ideally, the sole of your boot should be roughly level with your horse's breastbone or a few inches either way when you are on top. Of course, we see lots of successful combinations which don't accord with this guide.

long legs Riders with long legs may inadvertently begin to grip up because of the feeling that there is nothing to wrap their legs around. Gripping at least produces something to feel with the legs, but the real answer must be to learn to ride with, and train the horse to respond from, the seat and upper legs. As the horse's ribcage rounds, it slopes in under the horse leaving nothing for the long-legged rider to make contact with from the mid-calf down. If you can ignore this fact and use your seat, upper leg and balance so that you are not actually trying to find your horse with the bottom part of your lower leg, you will do much better.

short legs Riders who feel their legs are too short often try too hard because they feel that the horse is not listening to them, they cannot apply strong enough aids or the horse is too strong for them. The strength of the horse, clearly, has nothing to do with the length of the rider's legs. Be that as it may, these perceived inadequacies can result in kicking, gripping up with the legs, driving hard with the seat, overuse of the reins and general over-activity. These riders need to work on developing a deep seat, perfect balance and using whatever leg is available in a relaxed and positive way.

50 Improving the stillness of your lower leg

I once saw a piece of film at a lecture demonstration about the Cadre Noir, the élite corps of the French classical academy at Saumur. One of the Ecuyers was performing lovely level one-time flying changes on one of the beautiful French Anglo-Arabs. With the horse on the weight of the rein, neither was throwing themselves around but the rider's lower legs were swinging loosely with each change. The lecturer said: 'You will note that the rider has such perfect balance and the horse is so light and accomplished that the lower leg is superfluous.'

What a difference from the kicking and kinking so often seen. When questioned on this point later, he explained that a rider able to perform such an air (movement) with such loose legs and seat was truly riding in perfect harmony and balance with his horse. The legs did not matter.

Unwanted movement of the lower leg

A lack of tone in the leg muscles and poor balance in the saddle are the two main causes of an unstable lower leg. It also seems to occur more in trot than any other gait. On the rise, in rising trot, the legs, or even just the feet, may flap outwards. If the leg movement is a back and forth one, this signifies that your balance is not centred and you are, perhaps unknowingly, using your knee as a fulcrum as you rise.

What can I do?

Remember: before you can achieve something (control) you have to be able to do nothing (looseness). Mastering a loose seat and legs is the first part of acquiring a controlled position without rigidity or stiffness.

In rising trot think of dropping your legs down through your heels and of pushing your feet down and together under your horse's breastbone every time you rise. To stop your feet from flapping backwards and forwards, work on improving your balance and gently push your heels towards your horse's hocks as you rise.

51 Maximizing leg contact

You'll probably be familiar with your instructor telling you that you must always give your aids with the inside of your leg and when you dismount there should be no grease from your horse's coat past the back seam of your boot. This is to encourage the rider to let the legs hang loose, down and around the horse's body maximizing contact for communication.

Toes sticking out

I really sympathize with anyone who has this fault because it's one of mine. I put it down to the fact that I did a lot of ballet dancing when I was growing up and it has permanently deformed my leg ligaments! The fault used to be much worse when I was dancing and I had to try very hard so as not to give my old riding master cause for his frequent complaints. It improved with time, so if this is your excuse too, there's hope yet.

Riding with the toes turned out can cause the legs to lose contact with the horse's sides followed by the knees turning away from the saddle, both of which cause a strain on the hip joints and predispose to gripping up.

What can I do?

There are several designs of flexible or hinged stirrups available which really help with this problem because they increase the comfort of your ankles, soften the weight and reduce jarring. Simply being sure to ride with the ball of your foot exactly along the tread rather than twisted across it also helps.

If pain in your ankles is a problem, try taking less weight on your feet and stirrups and take it on the insides of your thighs instead. Practising rising trot without stirrups will help you get used to this – keep

the legs loose and don't influence your toes, then when you take your stirrups you can spread the weight more easily. This is also excellent for maximizing your contact against the horse's side. Other exercises such as circling the

ankles will help to get rid of stiffness.

Some trainers believe that your knee and toe should be slightly turned out when riding – as long as your legs are relaxed and long, just do the best you can and don't worry about it.

Legs

52 Improving the effectiveness of your leg aids

A very common complaint is 'my horse doesn't listen to my leg'. Effective leg aids are obviously a big help in riding! If a horse ignores the rider's leg it is usually – not always – the rider's fault because the leg is used all the time, either pressed on constantly or used at every stride. Such aids desensitize the horse, he becomes 'dead to the leg' and lightness becomes an impossible dream.

Nagging heels

Riders often ask for forwardness by constantly asking the horse with the legs believing that their horse will stop if they don't keep at him. However, the problem of nagging heels often occurs because most horses are never taught to utilize the exuberant, free and forward movement from youth and get into the habit of trundling along nonchalantly. But feeling forced to nag the horse constantly with your heels or lower legs does not justify the problem.

Mild, gentle nags with the heels are worse than useless because horses can easily tolerate them and do not respond because they are a constant, meaningless part of being ridden. The horses therefore become dull and unresponsive to ride. I should imagine that they find nagging slightly irritating which cannot help their attitude to work. Few horses are ungenerous or lazy by nature but get worse with constant nagging.

84   RELATED AREAS OF IMPROVEMENT   **50**   **61**   **73**

What can I do?

When loose in the field, the horse moves quite leisurely with spurts of speed when playing or skirmishing. Under saddle, we aim to reproduce his natural gaits but the horse finds it more difficult because he is now carrying around a sixth of his own weight – a moving, possibly unstable and interfering weight at that. We therefore have to educate him as to an effective way of going and a safe posture for carrying weight.

Initially he needs to go with both ends down and his middle held up for appropriate muscle development. Ultimately, he needs to learn to go with thrust (impulsion) from his hind legs and quarters, with his back and belly up and with his head and neck held up and pushed forward in self-carriage. This impulsion and forwardness is created by the rider's legs but without nagging constantly with your legs.

To get out of the habit of nagging at your horse's sides while he walks on resolutely, try the following approach: Next time you ride, aim to perform a loose, free and active warm-up walk on a long rein. It doesn't matter whether you are in an arena or out on a hack. Get him going with slightly more emphatic forward aids than you usually give, which might surprise him. Push forward smartly with your seatbones without bouncing up and down in the saddle. Use your legs actively (try not to kick back) in definite inward pinches or taps immediately behind the girth.

Encourage him with your voice to 'walk on', if necessary move your whip up and down his side or hit your boot with it, but only flick him with it if he is just not responding. When he is going at a smart walk, praise him verbally, stop using your leg aids but do keep following his movement, not too exaggeratedly, with your seat and hands to tell him, in classical parlance, that he is to keep going.

He will slow down fairly soon because he is not used to marching instead of ambling. Remind him with the same aids and as soon as you get the walk you want praise him, stop the aids and just sit there, going with him and enjoying it. You must be really firm with yourself to not use your legs again until he slows down.

This technique works with all gaits. The horse will soon learn (one lesson or two at the most) that every time he back pedals you will chase him up – and it must be every time – so instead of thinking about slowing down he expects your command, and forwardness becomes the norm. In this way, your horse will learn that forward means forward, and may well prefer this to being nagged.

53 Improving your leg position

A riding teacher using classical principles will encourage the student to gently push the hip joints, or some say the tummy, forwards slightly in the saddle. This promotes a steady seat with the rider on the seatbones rather than on the fork or buttocks and slightly flattens the small of the back so that the rider is not riding hollow backed. This is the foundation of a good riding position on the flat.

Legs too far forward

The legs cannot act effectively when they are forward of their correct position. Looking at such a rider from the side, the vertical straight line from the ear, through the shoulder, hip/elbow and finally the ankle joint is broken at the hip and angled forwards. If a rider sits with their legs forward in a well-balanced saddle, they may feel the need to counteract this heavy weight forward of their centre of balance by bringing the shoulders slightly forward, which usually drop along with the chest, and sticking their bottom out behind. In this position, very few riders maintain slight muscular tension down the back, but allow the whole torso to go slack. This reduces upper body strength, control and the entire balance. It also can put a strain on a weak back because the muscles are being used not to hold the torso erect, but to actually hold it up against gravity and the movements of the horse. In addition, the arms are usually taken too far forward which has two main effects. It further weights the top part of the torso and pulls it forwards along with the shoulders, and it affects the contact with the horse's bit.

Some riders with forward legs sit on their buttocks with the upper body back and the hands too high. This can occur because the saddle is too far

RELATED AREAS OF IMPROVEMENT   **1**   **25**   **46**

forward, almost on the tops of the horse's shoulder blades, tilted up in front and throwing the rider back on to the cantle. Other reasons could be that the stirrup bars are too far forward, pulling the legs with them, or that the saddle has an extended, rear-inclined seat like the old British and Irish showing saddle design.

What can I do?

1 Ensure your saddle is far enough back on your horse so as to not interfere with the shoulder movement. The shoulder blade swivels around a fulcrum point about one third of the way down the bone, between the top of the withers and the point of the shoulder. On the ground, when the foreleg is extended forwards to the point where the top of the shoulder blade swivels back, you must be able to fit the side of your hand between the top of the shoulder blade and the front of the saddle. Check that the back of the saddle does not extend beyond the horse's last rib. If it does, the saddle is too long for the horse's back.

2 Ask a knowledgeable friend or teacher to check your position at halt, paying particular attention to the straight, vertical line ear-shoulder-hip/elbow-ankle. Hold yourself, definitely but not rigidly, in the classical seat, described on pages 8 and 9, with emphasis on keeping your ankles back and your hip joints forward. This will feel awkward at first! Relax into this position and then try it in walk, ideally on the lunge, and progress from there.

3 Try these dismounted exercises: Sit on a hard chair and place one hand under your bottom and find your seatbones. It is this part of your seat that you need to sit on when in the saddle. Stand erect and tuck in your bottom, then push your hip joints forward without force or strain, hold, relax and then repeat.

One situation when it definitely helps to have your legs forward is coming down from a drop fence across country (see photo above). You do have more chance of staying on in this position as your legs will brace against the upward force felt on landing, but you need very good balance as you need to get back to your normal position on landing whilst the horse is adjusting his own balance, too.

However, the author does have some old books containing fascinating photographs showing the Italian cavalry of around 100 years ago coming down the near-vertical slide at the cavalry school, Tor di Quinto, with not a forward leg in sight!

Legs

54 Strengthening your lower leg

Speaking generally, the best place to hold the lower leg is more or less vertically to the ground, with the ankle bones beneath the seatbones and the toes underneath the knees. This applies to jumping, too, except for drop fences when many people find a forward leg more reassuring and effective at keeping them on.

Legs too far back

If a rider is anxious to get the horse to go forward and so leans forward, the legs often go back at the same time. A badly balanced saddle could also tip a rider forward. A few dressage saddles are still made with quite a high cantle which, without being balanced by the pommel, can push the rider forward – and if the rider leans forwards, the legs often go backwards.

A horse with a high croup or 'downhill' conformation often has the effect of tilting the rider forwards slightly, which may tempt the legs to swing back as the upper body goes forwards. This conformational fault has different effects on different people – some will compensate for the forward and downward force by putting the legs and feet forward, stiffening them and bracing themselves against the stirrups.

The most sensitive area in which to give an aid is immediately behind the girth. Although the legs will probably be further back than this, if the legs make a significant contact some horses will take this as a constant aid to go forwards and will rush off or simply go faster than the rider wants. As this posture means the rider is not in a well-balanced, secure position, particularly if the upper body is tilted forwards as well, this can frighten many riders and cause them to

88   RELATED AREAS OF IMPROVEMENT   **2**   **45**   **49**

bone is not directly underneath the seatbones, so the weight does not fall straight down. The knees tend to become a fulcrum around which the rider pivots and the lower leg, as well as being too far back, becomes stiff. To complicate matters further, the leg is, in practice, 'shorter' than when it is dropped down correctly from the hip, so the rider's stirrups may well drop off the downward pointing toes.

What can I do?

To correct this fault arrange some lunge lessons in which particular attention is paid to the correct seat and establishing better balance from a loose seat and legs. This will help the rider to sit up from the waist and drop straight down from the waist, to balance on the seatbones and let the legs hang straight.

To check that your legs have not slipped too far back again, glance downwards over your knee without leaning forwards – you should just be able to see your toe in front of it.

grab the reins in an effort to stabilize themselves. Unfortunately, they often grip with the legs too, making the problem worse.

From the rider's point of view, legs which are held too far back are usually held so from the knee and are accompanied by raised heels and toes pointing downward. It is very difficult to maintain a low heel with the weight dropping down through it in a leg which is too far back because the ankle

Pushing the right button

There are four positions on the horse's side which classical author, trainer and teacher, Sylvia Loch describes as buttons. They are fairly precise points which the horse is pretty adept at working out for himself – probably because, like the other classical aids, they are logical.

For clients still getting to grips (not a good pun) with leg positions, I am happy for them to use just two positions – Button A which is on or immediately behind the girth and Button B, set a little further back, for lateral work and curves.

Many people give leg aids too far back. Usually, the leg is raised up and back from the knee and the rider jiggles with the heel. Often when this fault is pointed out to a rider, and the correct leg position shown, it will 'feel' wrong. Years of habit not only produce comfort, but are hard to eradicate – like many aspects of riding you just have to get this technique into your 'body memory' or proprioception. Once you discipline your mind to think about what you are doing, you will achieve much better results.

55 Correcting your stirrup length

The ideal stirrup length to start with is fairly easy – when you are mounted let your legs hang naturally straight downwards and adjust the stirrup so that the side of its tread is level with your ankle bone – not above it or below it, just level. When standing in your stirrups, your fork should just clear the pommel of your saddle as shown top right on page 91.

For jumping, shorter stirrups push your seat back in the saddle and give you an altered balance, enabling you to lift your seat into the jumping position through some leverage from your thighs. Most people are happy at a jumping length of three or four holes shorter than their flatwork length.

Inappropriate stirrup length

Many riders feel most secure with their stirrups a little too short, say one or two holes. This does give a certain amount of 'body leverage' and reliability of balance if you are riding a horse that messes about and takes a hold – just until you re-school him, of course! Other people have read so much about a 'classical long leg' that they try to ride with stirrups too long as they strive to achieve what they believe to be a classical seat. This is shown in the middle picture on page 91. The rider is tip-toeing and the heels are up, a common result of too long a stirrup length.

RELATED AREAS OF IMPROVEMENT   **9**   **12**

What can I do?

flatwork Take your feet out of the stirrups, spend a few minutes stretching from the hips and let your legs hang down naturally. The bottom of your stirrup should be level with your ankle bone, allowing you to lift your toe into the stirrup without shortening your leg.

jumping To find out why shortened stirrups are normal and preferred for jumping fences, all you have to do is try jumping them with normal flatwork-length stirrups even in a properly forward-cut jumping saddle. It is difficult and uncomfortable. You cannot get your balance right, the stress on your upper thighs is pretty

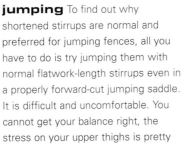

awful and you feel that you cannot lean forward or fold down properly. To find the correct jumping length, shorten your stirrups three holes from your flatwork length and move into your forward position. If you find it difficult to balance when standing still, you will find it impossible to stay balanced when jumping. Adjust your stirrups further until you feel comfortable and your lower leg feels secure, with your toe below your knee. This rider (left) has put a bridge in her reins by taking both reins in both hands. The rider can use the resulting doubled-up portion of the reins that pass over the horse's neck as a 'bridge' to stabilize her balance, but should not use it to lean on.

56 Refining your leg aids in canter transitions

To ask a horse for canter, first establish a good working trot, sitting. The place at which it is easiest for the horse to make a canter transition is in a corner of the manège where he has the fence all round supporting his outside. To warn the horse that you are going to ask for canter, a few strides before you reach the corner, place your inside seatbone forward, more so than if you were simply circling, and keep it there.

Too much outside leg in canter transitions

When a rider is anxious to obtain canter, it is easy to exaggerate the familiar aid of outside leg back, on and go. Frustratingly, of course, the 'go' doesn't always happen. By using too much outside leg, a rider can throw a horse off balance, bring the quarters in maybe to the extent of forcing the outside hind to cross over the inside one just as it is coming forward and – well, you can imagine the result. I have seen horses stumble badly through getting their legs tangled up because of such a crude aid. If the horse does pick up canter, he will be going quarters-in for a few strides and, although he will straighten himself up, he will be unbalanced for several strides.

What can I do?

The use of the outside leg to obtain canter is known as the diagonal aid. Horses which are schooled to go from the inside leg are said to go from lateral aids, for obvious reasons. Lateral aids have long been regarded as being more advanced, more subtle and more effective, with the outside leg just being placed back but not actually put on, to remind the horse not to swing the hindquarters out. You can give an aid (a tap or a squeeze) with the outside leg to ask him to pick up canter with the outside hind (the leg which starts the first stride of canter) and with the inside leg to ask for forward movement.

If it is your tendency to use too much outside leg in canter transition, tell yourself that your outside leg has no use in it and that you are schooling your horse to go from lateral aids – and do so. Approach your corner in exactly the same way but just position your outside leg rather than using it, or even just leave it to its own devices when you push your inside seatbone forward. It will probably go slightly back of its own accord. Give an inward squeeze or tap with the inside leg and/or lift the inside seatbone along with the other aids, particularly the verbal 'canter', and I am sure your horse will canter willingly. Don't forget to praise him when he does.

In the corner put your outside leg slightly back, your outside rein pressing lightly sideways on the neck just in front of the withers, your inside leg down, supportive, still and held immediately behind the girth, and your inside rein held slightly up and in towards the centre of the curve (which you regard as part of a circle), asking for a slight inside flexion so that you can just see the corner of his eye and the outside of his nostril. As your outside leg goes back, say 'canter'. A well-schooled horse should go into canter from just a forward lift of the inside seatbone. Any horse who understands seat aids and has reasonable self-balance in canter should be able to pick this up as a progression of lateral leg aids which, themselves, progress from diagonal aids.

57 Stabilizing your leg when jumping

If you watch any show-jumping class you will see many different weird and wonderful jumping seats, some of them displayed by successful riders who seem to have amazing natural balance. For most riders, though, a still, vertical and stable lower leg, with the weight dropping down through a flexible ankle, is the most secure position to adopt.

Legs flailing when jumping

Poor balance can cause a rider's legs to flail when jumping as too much weight is tipped forwards as the horse jumps. This is extremely common when riders tackle larger jumps than they are ready for. Over active legs can also occur when a rider has a problem with producing free, forward movement in the horse and constantly kicks out of desperation to clear the jump.

What can I do?

If you suffer from flailing legs when jumping, the first thing to do is to go back on the lunge, without reins or stirrups, and practise sitting on the seatbones in the flatwork position

with a loose seat and legs, and become confident of staying with the horse in all gaits. Balancing exercises on the lunge such as holding the arms horizontally and vertically and circling them are also helpful.

From here, progress to tackling a grid of low fences or cross-poles at even distances, again without reins, and if you are brave enough, without stirrups. Once you can stay balanced over low fences, canter the horse while in the jumping position over undulating ground, with or without stirrups, and on a fairly long rein, so that it is there for control if necessary, but not for the rider to hang on to. Once the horse and rider can do all of this, few fences in competition should cause this problem to resurface provided they start competing at an appropriate level and build up sensibly.

Effects of fitness, tone and suppleness on the rider

Unfortunately for riders, riding is not enough to acquire the fitness and strength to enable you to become an athletically competent rider. If you stop riding for a while you often notice stiffness and a physical weakness creeping in, not to mention a lack of cardio-vascular fitness. You may not be saddle sore, but you will probably feel stress or strain in the seat and groin area and your knees may feel weak when you dismount. Unfortunately, the older you get, the worse this becomes.

Your cardio-vascular fitness is also very important, it's surprising how out of breath you can get after just a few minutes warming up and working-in in trot. Brisk walking, jogging or running are all effective, as are skipping, swimming, step exercises and cycling. Strength training, particularly for the legs and the back/torso are important for riders. Try resistance training, some work with weight bands on ankles and wrists, and stretching, especially for the legs. Yard work, of course, is excellent but still not enough, you really need a structured routine.

Try something a little different

pilates The Pilates method, pronounced pi-lah-tees, (named after Joseph Pilates who developed it) is a gentle form of exercise and body control which improves fitness of the body and relieves mental stress. Its main principle is to strengthen the postural muscles which stabilize the torso and improve the balance – essentials for good riding.

yoga An aspect of ancient Indian Ayurvedic medicine, yoga assumes that all systems of the body, mind and spirit work best when in harmony and balance. The body's energy flows round channels or meridians in the body which can be stimulated and manipulated by special stretches and postures. Tension, tightness and stiffness are counteracted by gently flexing and lengthening soft tissues and joints, circulation of body fluids is improved, the spine becomes more flexible and resilient and the back muscles become stronger and more elastic.

tai chi An eastern therapy, Tai Chi involves graceful, flowing movements which work with the body's energy flow to enhance the development and maintenance of health and well-being, regulating the system, preventing disease and strengthening the mind.

the alexander technique Devised by F. Mathias Alexander, this technique improves co-ordination, performance and well being in the rider and, consequently, the horse's performance and attitude. Most of us sustain injuries during our lives which can cause our bodies to compensate for the pain by moving in an 'avoiding' way, using the wrong muscles. Good posture involves reflex responses which we can over-ride when in pain: the Alexander Technique can help us to learn to stop interfering with them so that we can restore their effectiveness and, so, normal movement.

feldenkrais Developed by the renowned physicist Dr Moshe Feldenkrais, this method is based on educating students to achieve postural awareness through slight and gentle, non-habitual exercises which aim to achieve efficient movement using the least effort. It removes mental and physical blockages in the rider and so helps prevent resistance in the horse and improves mental, spiritual and physical communication with him. The horse is freed to give his best performance without hindrance from the rider.

Readers are referred to the author's book *Complementary Therapies for Horse and Rider* (David & Charles, 2001) for further information.

Non-communication

Clear thinking

Dealing with any living creature is obviously all about communication. You tell them what you want them to know and they tell you what they want you to know. Unfortunately, when dealing with animals many people, even now in a supposedly enlightened time, do plenty of the first but don't consider the second. Even when they do take in what their horse is communicating to them, if it's not what they want to hear, they often ignore it.

By nature, horses rely mainly on body language and, it seems fairly clear, some as yet undefined sixth sense to communicate with each other. Horses are not very vocal animals, certainly by our standards, so although their hearing is extremely acute, they seem to use it, as prey animals, more for detecting sounds in their near and far surroundings than for listening to each other, although they do the latter, of course. It is interesting to watch horses communicate with each other and with other animals. They all seem to understand each other perfectly, as though they all have some common language unknown to us, a species apart. I am sure, from my own experiences and observations, that animal language is made up of body language and what is commonly called extra-sensory perception (ESP) – extra, not because it is in addition to, but outside the normal five senses. It has been put into this category because there is no obvious sensory organ by means of which this sort of communication can be detected or described.

It has been suggested that young horses try to communicate with humans as they do with their dams and field mates, but soon learn that it is not being understood and so give up. This gives them their first confirmation that we are not 'one of them'. Some humans certainly do pick up on these ESP messages even without trying. I have experienced several instances of it from my dogs and my horses. I have already described in this book how important it is to think to your horse what you'd like to do and, if you are clear in your thoughts, your horse almost always does it.

Are You Listening?

An arrogant, independent old Thoroughbred mare I bought about ten years ago, Sarah, started communicating with me after about six months. After having got used to this, I tried it with her one day for a direct request: 'Please would you deign to come over here?' Not a twitch. I tried again. Nothing. The third time, I asked hard in pictures for a full half minute and in the end she turned round with an unsurprised 'now what?' look on her face and sauntered over. She was above titbits and would have regarded a rub on the forehead as degrading, but accepted a stroke on the neck and an ESP thank you. Years later, I went to the field to bring my two horses in at dusk. They both watched me arrive at the gate and I shouted to them. They looked over to each other at the same moment (they were far apart) for several seconds, apparently discussing the matter, then they evidently agreed that coming in was OK and started strolling over at the same time from their different directions.

I know that this book is about improving riding faults and this particular section might well have been expected to be about correct physical aids but I feel that ESP (for want of a better expression – can anyone think of one?) and more effective communication is so important with all animals, but particularly with prey animals as sensitive as horses, that to not give it more emphasis than normal would be foolish. Members of The Equine Behaviour Forum (see page 150) regularly submit articles and letters describing their experiences on the subject and offering their views – I do not think the existence of some sort of ESP can be denied. Let's make more use of it for all our sakes.

58 Maximizing the use of your voice

Horses are sensitive to sound of all kinds and it has a great effect on them. As prey animals, they use mainly their eyes and their ears to spot predators as far off as possible. A rustle in the grass, the crack of a twig or the far-off sound of a group of predators making their way closer are all picked up and acted upon.

Ideally horses should be trained with consistent voice aids from earliest foalhood and the precise commands passed on to their purchaser so there can be no confusion. But, of course, this isn't an ideal world. If horses were trained this way, the specific words could be used in the stable, field, in-hand, on the lunge, while long-reining or loose schooling and under saddle.

Incorrect use of the voice

For such a vocal species as ourselves, we seem surprisingly lax at using our voices to communicate with our horses and, particularly, to praise them. Too often we give a vocal command, with or without other body language or physical contact aids, but take the desired result for granted, forgetting to praise the horse.

What can I do?

It's never too late to teach horses new things and they learn very quickly if the trainer is consistent, quick and fair. All horses should know the following basic vocabulary or something similar to get the intended response:

Stand (or Whoa)	*Over*	*No*
Good boy/girl	*Walk on*	*Back*
Trot on or Terrot	*Come here*	*Canter*

I firmly believe that all horses should know their names and come to call as easily as a well-trained dog. Circus horses are trained to do this and driving horses are worked by their names, so why are riders cheating

themselves? Other words or sounds are also helpful and horses soon catch on to their meanings. The horse in our photo is responding to the word back combined with a push on the breast. A long drawn-out 'easy' or 'alright' is very calming and can slow down or stop a horse. Maybe it's the actual wavelength of the sound which has the effect of calming or livening up a horse, but the way a word is said definitely makes a difference.

Most of us do chat to our horses in affectionate moments, but this is not normally a good plan when we want a specific response. For instance, if you

want a horse to stand who is messing about it's much better to say STAND firmly (without shouting or screaming) than 'I won't tell you again for goodness sake will you stand still when you're told I'm getting really cross...' and so on. You need to give clear, identical requests for each specific thing you want your horse to do, and you need to praise the instant the horse complies. Be quick to correct with 'No' and to praise with 'Good boy' or 'Good girl' so that the horse associates the sound with the deed and has clear parameters, as in a herd, as to what is accepted or wanted and what is not.

59 Disciplining your horse correctly

At the time of writing this, there is much discussion, at least in the UK horse world where the author lives, about applying discipline, or not, to horses. There is a variety of trainers and teachers of more different schools of thought than in previous decades and, in some quarters, a much more scientific approach to horse behaviour and psychology.

There are also many trainers using methods which are based on natural equine herd behaviour. If you spend time objectively observing a group of horses together, you will soon notice that they set each other very clear boundaries of behaviour.

Applying the correct discipline

There is a school of thought which believes that horses should not be corrected, and definitely not punished, when they do something which we do not want them to do. Instead, they must simply be praised when they get it right so that they want to do the right thing in order to get the reward (sometimes food, sometimes praise). However, not correcting them often results in a horse as objectionable as an undisciplined young, or not so young, human.

What can I do?

Setting aside the question of 'dominance' for now, horses who do something to a herdmate which that individual does not want usually get told about it in no uncertain terms with teeth or feet. Conversely, if a horse does something pleasant to another, the second horse may well do something pleasant in return, such as mutual grooming. Because this system is so clear, it makes sense to use it in our training and handling. I have always found that if a horse understands 'no'

for something unwanted and 'good boy/girl' for something wanted, and these parameters are applied instantly, consistently and fairly, horses become more secure, confident and co-operative because they know where they stand, as in a herd.

A notable exception to what I call normal discipline is clicker training,

which can achieve brilliant results using only praise. This system rewards the horse with a click and treat the instant the desired behaviour is achieved – something which many horses adapt to extremely quickly. If you want to try a new method, such as clicker training or positive reinforcement – consult a professional for correct instruction.

60 Helping your horse on the bit

Once a horse has learned to go forward willingly and calmly and to maintain a rhythm in each of his gaits (the rhythm being his natural movement, neither slacking nor rushing), he can be asked to come on to the bit. The need for this is to get the horse to realize for himself the best posture in which to hold and use his body in order to carry weight safely.

The expression 'on the bit' is one I avoid using as I think it gives the impression of the horse going down on to his bit with some pressure. I use the older expression 'in hand' which is much lighter in feel and gives an impression of partnership, give and take and comfort. Another expression is 'to bridle' which means the same – the horse going forward to his bit and accepting it without displeasure, holding it confidently and lightly, playing with it a little, using it as his forward boundary and as one means of communication with his rider.

Inability to get the horse on the bit

I find that one of the most common and unpleasant faults in riding today is riders who purposely haul their horses' heads back towards their chests in the mistaken belief that they are then on the bit. Others try too hard and ride with a harsh, even contact on both reins, which the horse himself may avoid by coming behind the bit. Neither of these situations is what a knowledgeable rider wants.

What can I do?

The horse must come on to the bit by working in the correct posture and pushing forwards from the hindquarters, never by the rider pulling backwards.

To strengthen the horse's muscles and posture, he needs to learn gradually to move holding his back and belly up enhancing the arched spine, his hind legs and hindquarters tilted under and pushing from behind, with his head and neck stretched forward – the poll should be just below or level with the withers

and the nose well in front of the vertical if he is a green horse or one unused to correct work. At the start of this work, the horse is learning forward movement and rhythm, and to accept some contact on the bit in his mouth but cannot be said to be 'on the bit' or 'in hand'. As the horse steadies in his work, the rider should take a firm but gentle and supportive contact on the outside rein to give the horse his 'space' in which to hold his head and

neck as described. By varying the subtle but definite contact on the inside rein, squeezing and releasing, the rider can ask the horse to relax his lower jaw. The inside leg tapping or squeezing intermittently immediately behind the girth asks for energy and for the horse to push his body forward to the bit.

If done correctly, the horse will give to the bit by slightly dropping his head and opening his mouth slightly (provided the noseband is not too tight)

RELATED AREAS OF IMPROVEMENT 26 28 61

develop the appropriate muscles and to start to learn an element of self-carriage. As he develops, the neck and head are raised gradually but the face should still be in front of the vertical.

working deep (bottom) is often confused with riding long and low, and is often used in more progressed horses. The back is still raised with the hindquarters and legs working actively under the horse but the nose is commonly held behind the vertical. This can cause the problems mentioned above in the poll and throat area. Deep work must only be used momentarily in specific cases by greatly skilled and sensitive trainers (a rare breed).

so that he is neither leaning on the bit nor holding or resisting it rigidly, but can slightly play with and listen to it. Although definitions vary, this is when the horse is considered on the bit (top). There is no leaning on it, pushing against it, resisting it or much champing of it. There are also no excessive amounts of saliva or froth, which indicate distress.

Short spells of work with rest periods will keep the horse's willingness to try, and eventually the horse will assume this new way of going. It involves some self-carriage and balance for the horse to hold himself without using the bit as a prop. This demands muscular strength which takes time to build up and the horse also has to get the idea mentally. Some horses with angular jaws, downhill conformation, thick necks and heavy heads cannot come into hand easily.

working long and low

The 'long-and-low' way of going asked of young and green horses (middle) is advantageous because it requires a raised and rounded back with the head and neck stretched low and out, but with the nose in front of the vertical, and the horse pushing forwards from behind. This posture makes it easier for the undeveloped horse to raise his back to learn to carry weight, to

Non-communication

61 Creating impulsion

Impulsion from a horse feels like energy flowing forwards beneath the saddle from engaged, thrusting hindquarters, up under your seat and into the forehand and, therefore, your hands where it feels like a soft, lively ball of energy. If you've ever driven a powerboat and experienced that surge which pulls you back in your seat then lifts you diagonally up and forward as the bow lifts and the propeller churns into the water – that is the same kind of feeling. The problem is that on a horse you have no seat supporting your back so you have to keep your own balance and go with the surge. It has also been described as like sitting on the crest of a wave rolling in to the beach.

Impulsion not speed

One of the most common confusions in riding technique is between speed and impulsion. They are not the same. A horse going at speed can have impulsion or not according to his riding and schooling. A horse simply going fast may not be easy to slow down or stop but a horse going with impulsion is controllable, if you can stay in balance with him.

What can I do?

Before you can hope to get impulsion, your horse needs to have made a certain progress with his education. The first thing your horse needs to learn is free, forward movement, then rhythm and then he can learn to come into hand or on the bit correctly and without force. Once the horse is in hand, all you need to do with your inside rein and hand is keep them lightly in readiness to ask again should that situation change. Keep your firm (not hard), still contact on the outside rein like a strong but comforting handshake, to help him to balance without propping himself up on the bit.

You need to ride from your inside leg into the outside rein – your inside leg applies inward and forward squeezes or taps, intermittently, to ask him to send more energy forward to the bit. Use your voice cheerfully and in a lively tone to encourage the horse and keep the whole scenario light and energetic, not demanding and forceful. It is important that the horse is not asked, made or allowed to go too fast. Speed is not impulsion. Keep the forwardness, rhythm and the pace controlled but energetic.

To direct the impulsion you've asked for ensure you maintain your balance so you do not get thrown backwards and jab the horse in the mouth. Keep a contact on the outside rein until the horse is sufficiently educated and strong enough to go in complete self-carriage. Let the horse 'come through' from the hindquarters and go forward by keeping the inside rein communicative but very light and praise the horse the instant he responds as you want, otherwise how can he know that he has done it correctly?

62 Perfecting your transitions

It is important to get transitions right because they affect the quality of the new gait and are excellent schooling devices for improving balance, paying attention to the rider, mental acuity, sure-footedness under weight and muscular development. They help to bring the weight back on to the quarters and lighten the forehand and help to slow down horses that rush.

Cannot achieve smooth transitions

A major cause of poor transitions and, therefore, poor performance in the new gait is the rider having asked for a transition to a different gait while the horse was going poorly in the existing one. The horse must be going well and in hand (on the bit) in one gait before you can expect a smooth transition to a new one. Transitions can cause riders other problems too. Nervous riders can become anxious because they are anticipating that the horse is going to throw his head up, turn his quarters in, flatten out, fall out through his shoulder and do a racing trot into canter and so on – because that is how the horse has responded in the past.

Other causes of poor transitions are lack of preparation, not giving the horse enough warning, indistinct or disorganized aids, harsh aids or lack of balance of either the rider or the horse.

What can I do?

halt to walk Have the horse standing well, in hand, and check your position. A classically trained horse (not necessarily advanced) should set off from a forward push of the seatbones, staying in hand and marching on. Do not push too hard or bounce in the saddle when asking for a transition – this will cause the horse to lift his head and flatten his back. All you need to do is remind the horse with vibrations or gentle squeezes of the inside rein to stay in hand just before giving the aid to walk. If your horse does not yet obey just the seatbones, ask with the inside leg immediately behind the girth (with a forward brushing movement) and do not hesitate to use your voice.

walk to trot Have the horse in a willing and energetic walk, in hand. Be sure that you are sitting correctly (stretching up from the waist, dropping down from the waist) and looking ahead. Some people like to prepare or warn the horse by giving a feel on the outside rein or simply by saying his name. Keeping the horse in hand, push forward with both seatbones – maybe using your voice as well. If this doesn't work, still keep the horse in hand, repeat and also brush, tap or squeeze with the inside leg immediately behind the girth. By asking clearly and decisively, but not roughly, you prevent the head flying up and the back flattening, and the horse will be more inclined to push forward smoothly from the hindquarters. As he trots, praise him.

trot to canter Have the horse in an energetic, willing and steady trot. Resist the temptation to lean forward which will lift and weaken your seat and encourage the horse to race-trot into canter – if he makes it at all. Sit upright correctly with seat loose and legs relaxed and down. Take sitting trot, following his back movements with your seatbones and absorb the energy in your lower back. Warn the horse of your wish to canter by putting your inside seatbone forward and, to ask a trained horse, just lift it. Use your voice if you wish. If your horse does not yet answer this aid, place your outside leg back from the hip to just behind the girth, and ask with your inside seatbone and leg. If necessary, ask with your outside leg, too. Many riders block the transition with the reins. Let your inside hand go forward a little or open the bottom three fingers, and do the same, a little less, with the outside hand to allow the horse to flex slightly inwards in the direction in which he is going.

63 Improving your rhythm and tempo

The correct rhythm and tempo is something a lot of riders cannot judge because they are told so often to send the horse forward and simply cannot tell when he is going too fast. It is quite possible for a horse to go faster than his balance can cope with because he thinks that is what the rider wants. He may not fall over, but he may well lean significantly on the bit to help him balance.

Rushing

Rushing is not comfortable to sit on, it can be rather frightening and a rushing horse is usually in a hypertense state which makes him susceptible to doing all sorts of silly things. Some horses use rushing as an evasion to get out of gymnastic work, others do it because they think that's what the rider wants as they are always being sent forwards. Horses are said to run away from pain. I'm not too sure about that always, but they do rush when they're unhappy about something to do with their work.

What can I do?

Have the mouth, teeth, back, saddle, girth, bridle, bit, feet and shoes all checked by professional practitioners. When you are sure he is physically OK, tackle the problem from the saddle – which I find is quicker and more effective than groundwork for this particular problem.

Next time you ride, get yourself into a really dozy mind set. You don't want to really go anywhere, you just want to meander around the school. Keep your seat and legs really loose and your upper body held up in relaxed muscular tone (but don't slop). Keep your reins loose or long depending on whether or not your horse is likely to shy and spook. Walk like this with a gentle contact for about ten minutes, warming up in walk, threading through cone patterns, up and down pole alleys, between jump stands – all very calmly.

When you're both nearly asleep, make a very casual transition to jog – jog, not trot. This is the point at which horses usually get into gear and go. If he trots ensure you stay relaxed and loose in the lower body and gently apply slowing aids and little circles until he's nearly walking. Keep applying the slow-down aids – intermittent tightening of the seat muscles only and immediately loosening them again, slight squeezes of the reins and stilling of the hands, and long drawn out vocal stop requests. When you achieve a calm jog, allow the horse to slide up to trot, still thinking slow all the time. If he picks up speed, do the same thing again to slow him down.

After a very few sessions of this, I am sure your horse will also have a non-rush mind set and you can progress his schooling, switching it on and off as needed.

64 Achieving the correct canter lead

To ask a horse for canter, place the inside seatbone well forward and weight it slightly, with the inside leg immediately behind the girth. Put your outside leg back and down from the hip. Your outside rein should be pressed sideways against the neck just in front of the withers (do not carry it over the withers) and your inside rein, with enough contact to ask for inside flexion, can be opened slightly into the bend.

Incorrect canter lead

It is quite common to see horses strike off into canter on the incorrect canter lead. This can be caused by the rider not giving enough of a warning to the horse of his wish to canter by putting the inside seatbone forward. It can also occur because the rider has leaned forwards, tipped sideways or leaned over into the bend encouraging the horse to trot fast rather than canter, cut corners, bank or motorbike, usually still in trot.

What can I do?

To ask for canter on a horse who normally strikes off on the wrong leg, you need to exaggerate the correct aids firmly but calmly so that he can be in no doubt. You also need to be certain that you are giving forward with the inside rein so as to not discourage the strike-off.

To increase your chance of success, ask for your canter transition as you go into a corner of the manège because the horse is controlled all along his outside by the fence.

You can also try on circles of varying sizes. Some people achieve success by letting the horse look slightly to the outside of the bend at first as some horses feel better

balanced this way (see above). You may achieve success by cantering a circle on the other canter lead, trotting for a few strides across the school and changing your position decisively and clearly before asking again. Remember to praise the horse the instant he gets it right.

65 Refining your canter aids

If the horse has been lunged correctly before backing and is accustomed to the normal vocal commands of walk on, trot and canter, he really should canter under saddle if the rider is sitting correctly and giving clear aids. The horse will associate the physical aids with the verbal aids and, if they are delivered correctly, calmly and decisively, he will canter!

The rider needs to sit erect and held in the torso with a loose seat and legs and must clearly warn the horse that canter will be requested by placing the inside seatbone forward (top right), applying the outside leg (a little back) and rein sideways on to the horse, and squeezing with the inside leg. Say 'canter' clearly. The best time to ask is when the outside hind, which is to start the canter stride, is stepping under the horse.

Cannot get canter

If you are experiencing difficulty getting your horse to canter have him checked by a professional. A sore back, poorly fitting saddle, sore feet, sharp teeth, ill-fitting bit or soreness in some other part of the body can all contribute to a horse's reluctance to canter. However, if your horse still won't canter, and you are certain that it isn't being caused by a physical problem, there must be lack of clear communication from the rider (above) – these may be confusing aids, no vocal request, or due to desperation and a subsequent loss of position in the saddle.

What can I do?

Invest in some lunge lessons on a calm and responsive horse. Have the aids for a canter transition clear in your mind and work on applying them quietly and clearly, without the worry of steering the horse. Once off the lunge, incorporate plenty of canter transitions into your schooling sessions. To make things easier in the beginning, ask for the upwards transitions in the corners of the school (bottom right). Once you have mastered this – pick a marker and be determined to get your transition at that point.

With horses who have a problem taking up canter, it often helps to let them look to the outside of the bend as this is how horses often turn naturally. Don't force an inside flexion but do raise the inside rein a little. If all these aids are clear and co-ordinated the horse will canter with practice and in time.

66 Improving your approach to fences

When it comes to jumping, the rider must concentrate on speed and steering and let the horse decide what to do with his own four feet. Make encouraging noises and keep him balanced, but don't tell him when to take off. Be quick to feel what he is doing, fold down instantly on take-off and look up and away to the next fence. Horses schooled like this are much safer and more likely to succeed than those dependant on their riders for guidance. No one is right all the time and if you make a mistake you will hinder the horse and get both of you into trouble.

Inability to see a stride

Many riders try to tell their horses how many strides to take coming into a fence and adjust the horse if he is half a stride out but, because they are unsure themselves and do not have a natural 'eye for a stride', give muddled directions, confuse the horse and get into real trouble. Trying too hard is often a cause of failure, not only in jumping, because it blocks mental communication with the horse.

What can I do?

A horse dependent on his rider for guidance will be unable to get himself out of trouble at a tricky fence, whereas a horse used to sorting himself out will take over, think quickly and probably negotiate the fence safely. Think of the old

saying: 'if in doubt, leave it out'. In other words, if you aren't sure what to do, do nothing.

To help your jumping become more natural and fluid, try using grids of jumps rather than concentrating on counting in strides to the point of take-off. Get someone experienced to set up a grid of fences with the distances set correctly for your horse. As you approach the jumps, remember to aim straight and pick a point in the distance, straight ahead of the last jump. As your horse jumps the grid try and look ahead at that point and simply fold down over each jump. As well as improving your jumping technique, these grids will help the horse learn to judge his take-off without relying on you for too much guidance.

Of course, it is useful to know how to control your horse's stride if you want to. There are several excellent books, old and new, on jumping technique and a well-recommended specialist teacher will be a great help.

67 Teaching your horse collection

The feeling a rider needs in collection is one of energy surging forward and upwards under the seat and into the horse's mouth where the bit directs and controls it. The horse feels balanced, light between the legs and in the hand. The horse should, in collection, be able to perform his movements without significant hand contact from the rider. To encourage the horse to rise into collection, use both legs, from their relaxed, down position, in a quick, simultaneous, upward pinching movement, stopping as soon as you get it, as always. Feeling collection under suitable instruction on an experienced horse is invaluable, giving the rider a true feel of the movement.

Cannot achieve collection

This is often caused, unpopular though it may be to hear it, by a lack of equestrian tact and sensitivity on the part of the rider, who may not be able to feel when the horse is ready or even asking to go in full balance from the hindquarters and 'lifted' in the back and forehand without reliance on the reins. It can also occur when a horse does not have the conformation or strength to carry himself in the necessary posture. Horses with tight, angular throats – that is a sharp angle at the throat rather than a loose, free curve – have difficulty in flexing from the poll and relaxing and opening the lower jaw to permit comfortable acceptance of the bit, without which a horse cannot truly collect.

What can I do?

Try riding a 15-metre circle in a corner of the school. Take sitting trot and use both legs in a quick, simultaneous, upward pinching movement – but holding the energy with the hands. You will feel the horse create more impulsion and energy which, instead of being used to go faster, will elevate and shorten each stride.

68 Teaching your horse to lengthen his stride

The most important thing to remember when asking for extension is that the rhythm must be maintained – the only reason for the increase in speed is the longer stride. The rider must be strong, erect and controlled in the upper body. The legs are used, in trot, alternately as each hind leg comes forward – for example, left hind coming forward, left leg squeezes immediately behind the girth. To allow the energy to surge forward, slightly open the bottom three fingers of the right hand (as your left leg is squeezing to encourage the left hind), and vice versa.

Cannot achieve extension

Many people are surprised when they are told that extension is harder to achieve than collection and that it is a more advanced movement, but that's quite true. Many riders find their horse simply gets faster and faster and increasingly on the forehand.

What can I do?

Muscular strength and balance is essential for good extension or even significant lengthening of stride. Lateral work and transitions are excellent preparation exercises to achieve this.

Horses often find lengthening and extending easier in trot because of the natural lift of the gait. Prepare with some leg yield, shoulder-in and walk pirouettes. Make sure the horse is on the bit and establish a steady working trot. On a long side or diagonal, sit up and hold the horse with your body. As you ask for lengthened strides, squeeze immediately behind the girth with alternate legs. Remember to give each hand as the horse lengthens his neck. This subtle finger technique is in no way to be compared with the harsh and exaggerated sawing movement often seen. It is a 'release-return'

movement with the fingers only of alternate hands. This technique is certain to produce lengthened strides in horses who respond to the leg. You can develop it from working trot into lengthened strides and from collection into extension.

The same principles apply in walk, provided you are sure to time your aids correctly – the walk is a lateral gait so the left leg squeezes as the left hind comes forward, followed

by the left fore/shoulder accompanied by a slight release of the left fingers, and vice versa. In canter simply ride forward, giving a two-leg aid in the moment of suspension and keep a contact on the outside rein while allowing with the inside one.

Remember, extension is an advanced movement for advanced riders! Gradual progression, concentration and a positive attitude will produce results.

69 Improving your rein-back

Rein-back is a mentally forward movement. It is not a backwards walk. The legs move diagonally, as in trot, but, of course, with no moment of suspension. When the rein-back has been achieved the horse must be asked immediately to move forwards again, staying in hand (on the bit) as he does so.

Rein-back problems

Common problems when trying to teach a horse to rein-back include the horse moving sideways, moving backwards but not straight, simply not going back at all, only moving the forelegs or throwing the head up and snatching the reins.

What can I do?

First, let's look at the aids for a rein-back. In halt lighten your seat by lifting your body a little and taking more weight on the inner thigh. You can also tilt your pelvis a little so that your seatbones are pushed back slightly. Place both legs down and back from the hips to behind the girth, resist steadily with the hands (never pull back as is so often seen) and then squeeze with both legs intermittently, giving the vocal command 'back' which the horse should know from the stable and work on the ground. When you get one step, praise the horse and let him stand. Then once more bring him into hand and repeat. Once he becomes more accomplished, replace standing with walking forward after rein-back to maintain forward thinking and impetus.

To teach your horse to rein-back establish a forward-going walk with the horse in hand, turn across the school and halt on the centre line. As soon as the horse stops, place both legs on

behind the girth, resist steadily with the hands and say 'back'. An assistant may help by gently pushing the horse back on the breast and stepping slightly towards his tail. If the horse moves his forelegs back but not the hind, it may be that you need to lighten your seat a little more or even lean very slightly forward. As soon as your

horse takes a step back, praise him and ask him to walk forwards. As you progress, ask for a few more steps of rein-back before asking him to walk on.

Start this movement with the horse in hand/on the bit, and intermittently squeeze one rein to maintain this if he shows signs of coming out of it.

70 Improving your horse's lateral work

Lateral work is valuable because of its suppling effect, freeing the joints, developing the appropriate muscles (the abductors and adductors which, respectively, move the legs laterally to the outside and inside) and expanding the horse's horizons by getting him to think laterally in both senses of the phrase. To prepare the horse, he should first be responsive to the leg when asking for turns on the forehand and haunches, he should respond correctly to a hand on his side and the request 'over' on the ground.

Cannot get lateral movement

The main problem encountered when learning lateral movements is simply that the horse does not move laterally. If you can get the feel of sideways movement on a light, willing and honest schoolmaster horse who knows his job and will help you whilst allowing for your mistakes rather than refusing to co-operate, you have a headstart. (You can save the tricksters for later when you have more experience.)

We normally prepare for the lateral movements by teaching turn on or about the forehand to obtain obedience to the leg (see photo on the right) and enable the rider to move the quarters and trunk. Once this is mastered it is not practised much as, to perform it, the horse must lighten his quarters and transfer weight to his forehand which is contrary to most riding.

After turn on the forehand has been learned, turn on the haunches (from the halt) can be taught to teach control of the forehand, and walk pirouette (the same movement from/in walk). These movements require the weight to be transferred more to the hindquarters.

Once you have control of both hindquarters and forehand, you should, in theory, have a horse who will move his whole body sideways in leg yield in which he flexes his head and neck

slightly away from the direction of movement which makes it easier for him physically. Half pass, in which the horse flexes towards the direction of movement is a more advanced movement and more difficult for the horse.

What can I do?

A good lateral move to start with is the leg yield, which many riders introduce after turns on the forehand and haunches. In the leg yield the horse moves both forwards and sideways, keeping his body straight except for a slight bend at the poll, away from the direction of movement.

To ride a leg yield, turn on to the inside track (about one metre from the edge of the school) which will allow the horse a couple of sideways strides to the track – enough to start with. Sit up, have your inside seatbone a little forward as you turn, straighten out on to the inside track for a few strides, then slightly weight your outside seatbone and 'point' that hip diagonally forwards to the track. Stretch your inside leg down behind the girth and with intermittent squeezes ask the horse to move laterally to the track. Once your horse can manage a few strides of leg yield, turn down the long side of the school at the quarter line to allow for a longer movement back to the track.

The horse failing to move sideways can be caused by incorrect or unclear weight placement by the rider as can be seen in this photo (right). Remember these key pointers:

1 Prevent the horse from just heading in a diagonal, straight line to the track by placing your outside rein firmly sideways on his neck immediately in front of the withers. As you give the intermittent squeezing aid with the inside leg, do say 'over'.
2 Ensure you almost drop the inside rein as even slightly too much contact on it will make it easy for the horse to fall on to the outside shoulder and just go straight instead of laterally.
3 Placing your weight on the outside, forward seatbone, dropping your inside leg down and squeezing, with the outside rein controlling the outside shoulder are the main aids for this movement.
4 Remember to look where you want to go. It is surprising how well horses follow your eyes as well as your weight.

Schooling techniques

It's up to you

It is important to look at all the usual reasons why a horse may not be complying with the rider's requests. The most obvious is discomfort or pain due to an injury, old or new, general body stiffness, badly-fitting tack, troublesome back, mouth or teeth or uncomfortable feet. Once these have been eliminated, the rider must take a good look at themselves; many riding problems are actually caused by faulty riding techniques which stem from a poor posture and seat. The position and posture described within this book are a fundamental basis to effective riding.

As for learning balance and technique, you still can't beat correct lunge lessons on a reliable lunge horse. The horse must be obedient to the trainer's voice and body language and must have steady, smooth gaits, must not fall in or out on circles and must have light sides for when the rider is allowed to start giving aids.

I find the easiest people to teach are those who possess good body co-ordination, balance and control. This can be natural or obtained through practising some other pursuit such as ballet, ballroom dancing, gymnastics or martial arts. Other practices which help greatly include yoga, Pilates, Alexander Technique and Feldenkrais. You do have to be fairly fit and supple with a degree of correctly developed strength to be an effective rider. Developing core body strength and control is the key. You must not allow your horse to throw your upper body around, in particular, because this is your self-carriage. Finally, mental and spiritual discipline is essential to anyone who wants to make progress and do their horse justice or who expects the horse to make an effort, too.

It is so true that your horse will take his example entirely from you if he has reason to trust you – trust that you will help him, not hurt him and not let him down. Bossy horses also need to know that they can trust you to fairly discipline them, as in a herd situation, otherwise they will, as in nature, take the upper hand. Reticent horses, similarly, need to know that they can trust you to fairly, confidently and clearly lead them, again as in a herd situation. These are not only matters of attitude but also of physical technique – using your body language and applying aids logically and in a way that the horse will respect, trust and understand.

Different teachers have different beliefs. My own beliefs are classical and, even within classicism, there are minor differences of opinion and technique. Classical riding generally teaches a loose seat and legs which hang down initially without stirrups, enabling the rider to learn to ride from and balance on the seatbones. This is nothing like so easy if the buttocks and leg muscles are contracted (toes held up or heels pushed down) and, therefore, to some extent rigid and stiff. It may not be possible to find a suitable classical teacher in your area but if you can find a helpful friend and a horse that will lunge well, you can do a great deal on your own. Try to keep your seat and legs really loose, your upper body 'held' and erect without stiffness, and you will find that on accomplishing this posture and balance you will be better able to give aids.

71 Learning to ride with the correct contact

It was perfectly possible 'in the old days' to educate and develop a horse to the highest standards without working behind the vertical. Horses have not changed significantly in their conformation, outlook or needs. Therefore, it is equally possible to do so now.

Horses forced to go overbent look distressed. You might get forward movement with an overbent horse but it will not be free – and freedom and *joie de vivre* are the very qualities sought in a properly trained and performing horse.

Overbent horse

Overbending the horse, which I think is the most obvious and common fault in riding today, is caused by riders not understanding the true principles of equine self-carriage. Constantly one is told that all but a green horse going 'long and low' must go with the poll as the highest point of his outline and with the front line of his face not behind the vertical. Overbending is exactly opposite to this – it can be caused by the horse trying to avoid the bit which, in turn, is often caused by riders' harsh and often deliberately heavy hand aids.

This is actually forcing the horse to go badly. In this position, the horse, because of his field of vision, cannot properly see where he is going. The nuchal ligament which runs from the poll down the neck and the horse's back, although very elastic, is not made to withstand such constant over-stretching, and the throat region can become very compressed as far as the salivary glands and the windpipe are concerned. Uncomfortable horses do not use other parts of their bodies well either. Often their backs are down, their hocks trailing, their forelegs flicking instead of arching out and their spirits squashed as can be seen from their demeanour.

What can I do?

A horse must be taught gradually how to carry his body in the most effective and balanced way. Once a horse has learned to go forward willingly and calmly and to maintain a rhythm in each of his gaits he can be asked to work in an outline. In the early stages of his training the horse's poll should be just below or level with the withers and the nose in front of the vertical. He will learn to accept the contact and gradually give to the bit by slightly dropping his head and opening his mouth slightly. He will be neither leaning on the bit nor holding or resisting it. Read page 100-101 for further advice.

72 Improving your horse's balance

As well as the rider needing good balance and body control, so does the horse. He is at a particular disadvantage because he is carrying the rider's weight, and if that rider also uses techniques which hamper him rather than help him, this makes his life really rather difficult. Experience under a good rider plus muscular fitness will help the horse, mentally and physically, to improve his own balance.

Horse is on the forehand

Riders often seem to blame their horses when they are on their forehand because they feel as though the horse is boring down on their hands and is heavy on the reins. However, like all the faults in this section, it is much more of a rider fault – although some horses with poor balance or downhill conformation will have a tendency to feel heavier in the hand.

What can I do?

This fault can be fairly quickly corrected if the rider gets the horse to propel himself from his hindquarters and simply does not let him lean on the bit. The easiest way to lighten the horse's forehand is to simply make the bit too unstable for him to lean on so that he has to learn to balance himself rather than relying on you for a prop. You'll be holding up a considerable weight in both hands, so squeeze firmly on one rein while releasing with the other. Try and squeeze the left rein when the left shoulder is coming back and release the right rein a little when the right shoulder is going forward, and vice versa. This will increase the forward, lighter feel you need – but do not pull backwards or 'saw'. This technique will

destabilize the bit and, combined with the leg aids, the horse will soon see that he has to learn to carry and balance himself.

To get a horse to propel himself from his hindquarters and engage his hind legs further under the body, the rider needs to use firm tapping aids with the inside leg immediately behind the girth, while maintaining a contact on the outside rein and giving and taking with the inside rein.

If the inside leg alone doesn't work, use both legs in an intermittent, firm and upward pinch movement immediately behind the girth. This should encourage the horse to raise his back and tilt his hindquarters under. If he ignores this, supplement it by a flick of the schooling whip to remind him that legs are not to be ignored.

73 Teaching your horse the forward ethic

The apparently lazy or sluggish horse is often caused by horses never having been taught to go forward and develop the forward ethic. Until a horse goes foward as soon as the leg or seat aid is applied, you cannot progress.

Sluggish horse

Many riders, particularly on horses at a riding school, struggle to get their horse going with impulsion and free forward movement. As a result, riders slip into the habit of constantly nagging at the horse's sides in an effort to keep him moving. I am sure horses must be irritated by this, but one thing is for sure, they don't regard it as a message to go forward. Many horses simply put up with the irritation and ignore it.

What can I do?

To rectify this problem the rider needs to sit up, drop the legs and balance correctly – and refrain from giving a leg aid with every stride the horse takes.

The way to create forward thinking is to sit up and keep the upper body out of the equation by remaining still, held and balanced. Give a sharp, inward tap or two with the inside of both legs, maybe reinforced by a flick or a wave of a schooling whip, plus the command 'walk on' until the horse understands and he goes forward into a smart march. Then praise him, stop all aids and sit quietly. The instant the horse back pedals, give the aids again in the same way and stop when you

get your result. Very quickly the horse will associate slowing down with being asked again in no uncertain terms to go forward. Once the horse is used to this way of going, just give the aid with the inside leg, keeping the outside leg there in support until needed for other aids such as turns or canter.

If the horse is habitually sluggish, you must consider clinical or nutritional reasons as to why he appears to have no real energy. Maybe he needs a change in his diet – perhaps something which will provide a little more energy. If things still don't improve and the horse's lack of energy is becoming a problem, ask your vet for a blood test (ask for an 'equine profile') which may reveal an underlying cause for the lack of energy.

74 Ensuring a pain-free mouth

As one of the commonest causes of head tossing is trouble with the teeth, put a note in your diary to get them checked if it is more than six months since they were seen to.

Head tossing

Horses that toss and throw their heads around are usually doing so because they have a problem in the mouth, with the bit (including the rider's hands) or their teeth. Others toss their heads as an evasion to get out of work. Some horses with short attention spans do it when they've had enough, some when they are hyped up by something close by (such as a butterfly or a herd of galloping colleagues).

Head tossing should not be confused with head shaking which often has its roots in clinical causes.

What can I do?

Firstly eradicate all possible sources of pain, in the mouth, ears and back, and check the fitting of the tack.

If the head tossing is bad enough to risk the rider being hit in the face by the top of the horse's head, for safety reasons a standing martingale should be fitted. Ensure it is fitted a hole or two longer than normal, so that it does not influence the horse's way of going, merely stopping him getting his head up beyond the point of control and preventing him throwing it around.

I often come across riders who, when a horse tosses his head or generally messes about, stop what they are trying to do, restore order and then start again. This tactic is soundly confirming to the horse that if he makes a fuss the rider will cease the demands and he can have a short

break. Deal with this problem, not by stopping, but by verbally reprimanding the horse and using strong leg aids to send him forward energetically. Praise him when he complies and give frequent breaks.

75 Respecting a light contact

To be able to ride a horse in correct self-carriage, and control, on the weight of the rein has always been the pinnacle of achievement for horsemen. A horse who bores, leans or pulls is using the wrong muscles in his work. Constant, good schooling and riding are a major part of correcting this situation.

Pulling

It is often said that horses pull against pain. I'm not too sure of that, but horses definitely pull and fight against restriction – and some have a good time taking off in a bit which they regard as no competition. I bought an old Thoroughbred mare some years ago who was completely uncontrollable in any kind of snaffle. In a stainless steel pelham (she hated rubber) she was a perfect lady for 90 per cent of the time, but she would not tolerate a double bridle.

What can I do?

One thing is certain, if you pull against a puller you will normally find yourself in a losing battle. It is better to let him pull against himself, if at all. If you bridge your reins (loop them from hand to hand over the withers, jockey style) and press the bridge down just in front of the withers, the horse will be doing just that, but that's merely coping with it, not curing it. Giving and taking on one rein alternately affords some control, and you need a really strong, secure and independent seat, back and legs to ride a horse like this.

I realize that the general theory is to bit a puller with a milder bit than his normal one, not a stronger one, but it takes a courageous and very skillful rider to effect a cure that way. From a general viewpoint, I have had success

in bitting pullers with a completely different kind of bit from the one they're used to. For instance, it is better to ride in a Kimblewick or a pelham than to keep using stronger and stronger snaffles. Some people swear by gags, but others claim that they make matters worse.

So is it possible to cure a puller?

My experience is that you can make things better with good schooling, but if suitable circumstances arise, he will revert to his former ways and pull. If you are faced with this problem, take heart in the fact that some of the top international riders have never cured it, just come to terms with it – which is something, at least.

76 Improving the horse's ability to work alone

The unwillingness of a horse to work alone is proof that the horse-human relationship is poor. The horse does not regard them as a mini herd and has no trust in or respect for his rider. The rider may be too weak, too tough or a source of confusion to the horse and this needs correcting before progress can be made.

Napping

A napping horse is one who refuses to leave the stable yard and/or his companions. Some horses will go so far, decide they've done enough and turn for home if they judge that the rider is powerless to stop them. Other terms for napping are jibbing and setting. Napping horses in the US are known as 'barn rats'.

Some horses are ungenerous by nature and learn to nap no matter how they are ridden. Others have been badly treated in the past, overworked, worked when in pain or sick or ridden harshly. Poor vision is another cause – something which is often overlooked. Horses in this situation deal with it by refusing to do anything.

What can I do?

Once this has become a habit, a horse will try it with anyone new. It needs a strong, fit, confident and knowledgeable rider to cope. Obviously, it's as well to try and discover why the horse is napping and to see if other techniques, such as groundwork by a trained person, could help.

Most old time horsemen, if there were any left, would tell you to move the horse strongly and rhythmically from side to side to break the mind set of planted feet. This rocks them off balance and often gets them moving. If you have the patience to just sit there and wait, a horse will often get bored and offer to walk forward. It is important to just sit quietly and every so often give the aids to walk on – if you get impatient and try to force the horse to move you'll only start a fight. Sometimes a napping horse will try and run backwards, rather than forwards. If this is the case, simply give the aids for a rein-back and encourage the horse to step back properly. Most horses soon decide that this is harder work than simply walking forwards.

77 Improving your horse's confidence

Fear, lack of respect, poor vision or lack of fair discipline can all cause a horse to lose confidence in his rider which can lead to adverse behaviour such as shying, spooking, napping and jogging. Over-feeding, under-working, lack of general exercise and turnout and under-exposure to the environment are other factors which may result in a jumpy horse.

Shying and spooking

Weak riding and wariness or nervousness of the horse being ridden can encourage a sharp horse to spook or shy unnecessarily.

What can I do?

If the shy is a very sudden one, you must rely on your deep, strong and independent seat! Any horse can shy without warning, but some are prone to it – by far the best way to protect yourself is to develop 'stickability' by means of working on your seat as a permanent part of your riding, as detailed elsewhere in this book.

If you see the spook coming, for example an unfamiliar object ahead of you, try and steer the horse's attention away from it by riding a shoulder-in or leg yield, flexing away from the object or situation, and riding strongly past it. A horse's natural reaction to something he doesn't really want to pass is to turn his head towards the object and swing his quarters around it – so the need for strong riding is important, especially if riding on the roads where you could swing into the path of traffic. If you are approaching a frightening object to your left, put your right leg strongly on and down from the hip just behind the girth, flex your horse round it to your right helped by a strong left rein

pressing sideways on the neck just in front of the withers and weighting your left seatbone. This will help to curve the whole forehand away from the object. He can still see it, of course, with his left eye, but your control and his posture should contain the situation. Keep insisting that the horse continues on his lateral path past the object with your leg and seat

aids. Really praise the horse all the time he is doing what you ask, calming and correcting him if he doesn't.

The horse may be genuinely frightened, but do not praise him if he is spooking and messing around. He needs to know that you are in control of yourself and him – so stay calm and firm with a 'good boy' and a stroke the moment you overcome the problem.

78 Improving your horse's straightness

The reason a horse needs to learn to go straight is to allow true distribution of energy and effective development of the right muscles and posture for riding.

Schooling techniques

Crookedness

Incorrect weight distribution is probably the main cause of crookedness. If the rider, who may genuinely think she is straight, sits more to one side than the other, the horse will incline that way. This can, in time, cause uneven muscle development in horse and rider, an out-of-balance saddle and maybe bruising and uneven gaits in the horse.

What can I do?

A knowledgeable eye on the ground is essential to tell if a rider is sitting and riding straight, when still and in action. The horse needs to be checked for uneven muscle development while the saddle should be checked for uneven padding and twisting.

To correct a crooked horse, it is better to bring the forehand in front of the hindquarters than take the easier way of correcting the quarters with the leg. If the quarters are to the right, press the left rein sideways on the neck just in front of the withers and press or tap the left leg on the girth to bring the forehand over. The reason for this is to keep the weight back towards the quarters rather than on the forehand where we don't want it.

An old concept to help acquire and keep straightness (on the straight or on curves) is 'the corridor of the aids'. The rider imagines that he or she is riding down a narrow corridor, the walls of which are formed by his seat, legs and the reins. If the horse is felt to

deviate one way or the other, he will hit the 'wall' – in other words the rider will block his sideways movement with the leg and/or hand, not hard but with a resisting feel. Slightly shifting the

rider's weight in the opposite direction to which the horse has deviated can also help to keep him straight. It is most important to maintain a straight torso and not to lean if the horse drifts to one side.

79 Helping relieve your horse's tension

If a horse is tense when ridden it will soon manifest itself in some way. Perhaps through tail swishing, the tail clamped down, grinding teeth or a lack of free-flowing movement. Anger is shown by a thrashing tail, a tight look to the face, ears often flattened hard back and down, an angry look in the eyes, nostrils wrinkled and sometimes the teeth showing. The horse may champ his bit excessively, the body may be tight and hard and the horse going unwillingly.

Old horses often have off days and young ones can be worked too hard by the over-enthusiastic owner, making them less than willing. Working a horse while his friends are in the field can cause understandable anger but must be overcome by firm but considerate riding to ensure the horse does not start to nap.

Tail swishing

Although this may not be a physical problem to the rider, it does indicate a tense or angry horse and we need to know why. Some horses justifiably express anger because they are being ridden badly – others understandably express it because they are being asked to do something they don't want to do.

What can I do?

We need to assess the whole situation before we can act accordingly. Start with tack, teeth, back, mouth and feet as being the most common problem areas. It does cost money, but in the long run it is well worthwhile calling in professional specialists to help. If the riding is at fault, the rider should take determined steps to improve and not ride that particular horse until he or she is more competent, because they will get nowhere together and if the horse becomes angry enough there could be real trouble. Some horses and people just don't even get on, let alone bond.

80 Teaching your horse to track up

Tracking up in trot, where the horse places his hind hooves in the prints of the fore hooves, is regarded as a sign that the horse is trotting well and using his hind legs and quarters to good advantage.

Physical considerations

Failure to track up can be caused by a conformational weakness. If a horse has a long back (as do many mares), he or she may simply not be able to stretch the hind legs far enough forward because the front ones are too far away. Other physical reasons for not being able to track up include a lack of suppleness in the spine and hips, maybe due to lack of gymnastic ridden work or bodywork such as massage and stretches. It could even be something more serious – perhaps the onset of arthritis.

What can I do?

If you have eliminated all of the physical reasons why your horse isn't tracking up, the problem is probably caused by the riding. To help a horse move forward in a balanced and energetic way the rider needs to sit correctly, deep and loose in the lower body and independent and toned in the torso.

Establish a decent working trot rising, neither too fast nor too slow, with a firm but comfortable contact on the outside rein. Ask someone on the ground to tell you whether or not your horse is tracking up. If not, use the same leg aids as for extended trot to encourage your horse to engage his hindquarters and legs and step well from behind. See page 112. If you find it difficult to give the alternate legs aids in rising trot, try it in sitting trot. Or, simply give an inward squeeze or pinch with both legs, immediately behind the girth, as you sit.

Do not use the alternate finger-release technique on the reins – just maintain a contact on the outside rein and keep the horse in hand with the inside hand, if necessary. Don't nag with the inside hand as this can impede forward movement and you want to initiate freedom and swing – only use it if the horse comes above the bit. Praise the horse the instant he co-operates.

81 Improving your horse's head carriage

A horse needs to work under saddle with his neck stretched in a forward and upward arch. Young and green horses still learning how to carry themselves are usually asked to go 'long and low'.

Head held too high

If a horse has been ridden with heavy, harsh and insensitive hands he will often raise his head to try and alleviate the discomfort in his mouth and neck. Other horses develop this head carriage if they have never been taught to work in the correct outline, or it may be a lasting habit from an old problem, such as troublesome wolf teeth or a bad back.

What can I do?

Before you start ridden work, give your horse a full medical check to eliminate a problem with his mouth, teeth, neck, back or feet.

I much prefer to deal with these horses without any training aids so that you get a true and lasting result – within a very few sessions. First of all, tack up the horse and stand beside him in his stable holding the reins under his throat about level with his chin. Give him a mint to get his mouth moving. Gently take up a contact on the outside rein and squeeze gently but clearly on the inside one, asking him to open slightly and relax his lower jaw, and saying 'head down'. The noseband must not be tight. Keep your hands about level with his chin. When he has finished his first mint, give him another. In about a minute, or less, he will give to your hand – instantly praise him, then let him rest.

Under saddle, do the same thing. Offer a mint, set off in walk with soft elbows and low hands. Hold the outside rein, pulse and squeeze the inside one and tap with the inside leg saying 'head down' and the second he does praise him and give him another mint. In trot you may experience more difficulty. Persist firmly, gently and calmly. With soft elbows and hands just below the withers use the same technique and give a squeeze from your inside leg. As soon as you get your result, praise the horse and stop the aids to reward your horse, resuming when the problem recurs.

82 Improving your horse's commitment to jumping

To present a horse to a fence correctly, always aim straight at its centre. Keep your legs down immediately behind the girth with your toe under your knee ensuring your stirrup is on the ball of your foot. Keep a steady leg contact and give him enough freedom of the head and neck, but don't drop the contact.

Running out at jumps

Running out is certainly a rider fault and not a horse fault. Run-outs are sudden changes of direction by the horse, not refusals. It can be caused because the rider presented the horse to the jump badly, usually crookedly, or because he or she did not give determined enough leg aids, allowed the seat and leg position to deteriorate and weaken in anticipation of a problem and did not keep the horse straight and in rhythm.

What can I do?

Check your jumping position – an observer should be able to imagine a straight, vertical line from the shoulder, through the knee to the toe. Keep the ankle really relaxed and let the heel drop down without allowing the lower leg to go forward.

To help prevent a run-out, carry your whip in the hand on the side to which the horse usually runs out. Often just seeing the whip on that side is enough to discourage a horse from running out. Keep your legs pulsing strongly for forwardness in time with his stride on the approach, with a little more pressure from the leg on his offending side.

Try presenting your horse to the jump in such a way that he cannot run out in his usual way. For example, if he normally runs out to the left, approach

the jump from the left on a straight diagonal line so you are jumping across it to the right. Alternatively, set up a jump on one side of the school with the fence on the side which the horse runs towards. Or use two jumping poles as extended wings to prevent a cheeky horse from diving out in either direction.

Of course, if you are getting constant run-outs at a particular kind of fence, take the horse back to basics and progress from there. This will help both of you improve your technique and confidence without worrying about the height of the obstacle. Gridwork is particularly good for horses that have developed a habit of running out.

83 Controlling your horse's jumping speed

Horses who rush round a course of jumps, often getting faster and more out of control towards the end, can be very frightening and also dangerous. The whole scenario of balance, rhythm and willingness to co-operate needs addressing. A firm, calm attitude on the part of the rider helps a lot – plus the ability to ride well! All the talent in the world is no good if you can't control the horse.

Rushing at jumps and on landing

Rushing is, perhaps surprisingly, caused by uncertainty on the part of the horse, or by excitement. Many riders approach fences too fast, getting speed rather than impulsion. On landing, the horse may charge off expecting a bang on the back as the rider tries to restore lost balance and comes down in the saddle too quickly.

What can I do?

The first thing to do is improve your own seat and balance. Gridwork is an excellent way to become secure over small to medium fences as you can concentrate on your position and technique without having to worry so much about steering.

In many cases a horse which rushes when jumping, gets excited at the mere sight of the jumps. To break this habit, school your horse in and around the jumps without jumping a single one. Keep everything very calm – as your horse relaxes, begin to ride towards the jumps and then simply circle away or change the rein. This will help break the association between jumps and speeding around the school. The use of placing poles in front of small jumps also helps to

correct a rushing horse – and guide the rider. Place a pole 2.75m or about 8ft 6in in front of a fence about 45cm or 1ft 6in high, approach it in a calm, active working trot and go with the little effort he will make (like a bigger

canter stride), then on landing, if he tends to speed away, bring him gently but firmly back to trot. Another pole the same distance away on the landing side will also help to steady the horse.

84 Improving your jumping technique

Jumping is all about confidence, and to have confidence you need to trust each other's standards of behaviour and level of professional skill. These are the foundations of a true partnership. There are lots of non-partnerships on the jumping circuit and they are agony to watch and, presumably, experience. On the other hand, mutual trust, ability and a shared commitment are ecstasy.

Refusing to jump

Many refusals are caused through a mistake by the rider. Often the rider has presented the horse at the fence wrongly, giving him no chance to jump. Sometimes preparation has been insufficient and the horse is over-faced. But the most likely scenario is that the rider, sub-consciously or more overtly, did not really want to jump, even if it was a sudden decision on his or her part and the horse sensed the reluctance and stopped.

What can I do?

If your horse has started to refuse recently, you must try and find out the cause. Check him for pain and discomfort first – tack, mouth, teeth, back, hindquarters and feet. If all is clear here, consider whether or not the horse has been sickened by too much jumping and especially over too many demanding obstacles. This is bad judgement on the rider's/trainer's part. Showjumpers practise infrequently at home and those still learning should only jump for a few minutes, several days a week, over fences of gradually increasing difficulty. The more difficult they become, the less they should be jumped.

An inexperienced horse with an

inexperienced rider is a not an ideal combination. The novice rider needs a confident horse that will pop over anything if set up properly. A young or green horse, on the other hand, needs confidence and guidance. Any kind of bad riding can contribute to a horse refusing – such as poor balance, hanging on by the reins, shaking the hands about, dropping the reins at the last second, banging on the horse's

back, jabbing him in the mouth or excessive use of the whip or spurs. The result is obvious and so is the cure.

Once all these causes have been dealt with, the horse can be started again from scratch. Pole work and tiny obstacles in all situations should re-establish confidence. In the long term, if the horse shows that he honestly doesn't like jumping any more, surely he could be found another job?

85 Learning how to cope when a horse bucks

A sensible plan is for any rider to learn how to cope with a bucking horse. Few people can stay on a determined bucker – even rodeo riders are not expected to stay on for more than a few seconds. Often, the first buck does the damage by unbalancing the rider and the second or third gets most people off. A few horses can buck with their heads up but it is more difficult for them. However, many bucking horses give up after a few attempts if they discover that it does not have the desired effect – provided they are not bucking through pain.

Bucking

Bucking as a means of getting a rider off is highly effective and usually caused by bad riding, past or present. Some horses buck because they simply don't want to be ridden, however well! Most do it because riding distresses and angers them.

What can I do?

First, check the horse's tack, mouth, teeth, back and feet for anything which may cause pain or significant discomfort and get it rectified. The second is to try, preferably under the eye of a good teacher or someone else who will actually ride the horse, to discover under what circumstances he bucks, what gait, transitions, which rein, what movements, which place in the school, in what tack, what kind of riding and so on. Then try to break down whether he has a problem or has simply learned that this particular evasion works. A re-schooling plan can then be devised.

If you are on a bucking horse – sit up, get the horse's head up and kick on. This may sound crude but this is an emergency. As soon as you mount, bridge your reins (see page 91) so if you are thrown forward the bridge will help to keep you on.

86 Learning how to cope when a horse rears

Rearing is regarded by most experts as the most dangerous thing a horse can do. All horses are capable of it, of course, but fortunately most aren't inclined towards it. If you know a horse has reared in the past, even once, my advice is just don't get on it. If you find yourself on a rearing horse, the most important things to remember are not to pull on the reins for fear of unbalancing the horse and bringing him back and over on top of you, and not to lean back.

Rearing

Its causes are harsh hands, sharp, severe bits insensitively used, persistent holding-in of the horse in the head and neck, extreme excitement, fear or anger. Many rearers have very sensitive mouths and have been made to rear by painful use of the bit or simply by firm pressure of any bit.

What can I do?

Immediate: If you have the presence of mind, lean forward and, if possible, put both arms round the horse's neck or hold the mane, staying as still as possible so as not to put the horse off his precarious balance. If you say anything, apart from praying, just say 'walk on'. As soon as the horse lands, move him forwards at once, and strongly, to prevent a repetition. Horses have to stop in order to rear so the instant you feel him stopping and gathering his weight on to his quarters say a stern NO, give him a very light contact and get him moving forwards as soon as possible. It is important not to punish the horse when he has landed as he may interpret it as punishment for coming down, or simply not connect the two happenings.

Long term: Expert and sensitive re-schooling, possibly in a bitless bridle, can be helpful. A simple rubber bit can be used or, in a true horseman's hands, a curb bit only (or a double bridle or pelham) with weight-of-the-rein contact. It takes a very competent rider with a completely independent seat and perfect control of hands and legs, plus excellent judgement of a horse, to re-school a rearer, but it is certainly possible. Some of today's natural trainers have had success in retraining confirmed rearers.

87 Eliminating resistance in your horse's mouth

If the teeth are neglected and sharp, it is possible for the cheek to be crushed between the back teeth and the bit's upper cheek or ring, causing an intense sudden pain. This can happen to a lesser extent even if the teeth are not sharp. Great care should be taken to see that the upper cheeks on curb bits are angled outwards a little, and that no bit presses against the horse's cheek in use. Other dental problems include wolf teeth and broken teeth, which can both cause trouble.

Throwing head up and hollowing

Some horses throw their head up as a result of sudden pain, or fear of one, in the mouth. Of course, when the head goes up, the back goes down and the hind legs trail out behind – complete disengagement. Many riders jab their horses in the mouth as a punishment for their own mistakes or overall ineptitude, or simply to stay on in certain circumstances. If the horse is frightened for his mouth, he may well keep the head up for some time or may go that way indefinitely, even after a change of rider, because he has no trust and fears more pain.

What can I do?

A veterinary surgeon or equine dental technician should check, and if necessary treat, a horse's teeth twice a year. The back should also be checked as a matter of course, because back pain from injury or a badly fitting saddle can certainly cause this problem.

Once any disorders have been corrected, and time allowed for recovery from any actual injuries, the bitting arrangement should be reassessed and a competent, sympathetic rider installed to effect an improvement through sensitive and knowledgeable re-schooling.

RELATED AREAS OF IMPROVEMENT   **22**   **24**   **63**

88 Learning how to cope if a horse bolts

Real bolting is not the same as a horse merely 'getting strong'. Bolting is terrifying and on a real bolter you are helpless. A farmer who had worked all his life with horses of all sorts once said to me: 'If you ever think you've stopped a bolting horse, you haven't. You've stopped one who has just finished bolting.' A sobering thought, but true. My feeling about a confirmed bolter is that it is not safe to ride.

Bolting

A true bolter is a horse in extreme panic who gallops 'blindly'. Some rider faults can lead to this such as causing the horse pain. The horse may be frightened or angry and once he starts galloping the flight-or-fight mechanism takes over and little but a massive obstacle will stop him.

What can I do?

If the bolting is an isolated incident, keeping the horse in plenty of work on a low energy diet may prevent a recurrence.

If you find yourself on a true bolter, what do you do? One crude method is to shorten your reins, take a firm hold, bring one hand down on to the opposite side of the withers to brace yourself, then pull upwards, hard and rhythmically on the other rein, alternating sides, if necessary. Another method involves turning the horse in a circle – you may not be able to stop him, but at least you can limit the distance you cover. Circling also often has the effect of calming a panicking horse – it gives it time to calm down and slow down of its own accord. Once the horse has slowed to a steady canter – you can think about bringing him back to a walk.

89 Learning to relax your horse

Aromatherapy oils can help to relax a horse (particularly lavender and lemon thyme oils) as can Tellington Touch and acupressure techniques – such as massaging the poll, or the traditional practice of stripping the ears (pulling them gently in the hands from base to tip). Some owners report success with various flower remedies such as Bach, Nelsons or the Bush range, available from health shops.

Grinding teeth

Grinding the teeth is caused by distress, nervousness, irritation, annoyance, apprehension or frustration and is sometimes accompanied by tail thrashing or swishing as well. There is no single rider fault which causes it – it can clearly occur due to any technique or situation which distresses the horse. Grinding the teeth is just one symptom of distress but it's a clear warning that all is not well. Mental tension and distress can cause other physical problems such as gastric ulcers, skin problems, cardiovascular disorders and general failure to thrive.

What can I do?

This is one syndrome which tends to disappear so long as the horse is kept, worked and handled humanely, suitably for him, and put under as little stress as possible. Some things which might worry a horse may be difficult to avoid such as farrier or veterinary visits, attending a competition, travelling, missing a companion and so on. At these times, understanding and sympathetic treatment is called for.

90 Establishing natural rhythm and speed

Schooling techniques

Agility and balance are key to a horse's performance and these can be enhanced by establishing in the rider and in the horse the horse's natural rhythm and speed at each gait. It may sound strange that the horse himself cannot recognize them but many cannot. Ask a skilled trainer to help you, then establish both for each gait in your head like a metronome.

Forgeing and over-reaching

Although this is fairly common in young horses or those out of condition, who do not have the co-ordination, balance and strength needed to avoid it under weight, it can certainly be caused by a rider who does not 'keep the horse together' and allows him to work too fast or in a strung-out posture. This is not the same as letting the horse warm up on a long or loose rein because, then, he is not being asked any questions.

Horses that have very short backs and those who are croup high quite often forge. It also occurs in soft or deep going because the horse cannot lift his front feet out of the way of his hind ones soon enough.

What can I do?

With maturity and patient schooling to improve balance and strength, the problem almost always disappears, even in horses that have poor conformation. In general, once the horse has been schooled to understand the different influences of the outside and inside reins, to respond to the leg and come in hand, he will be able to carry himself in a more balanced way and in a suitable posture to carry weight. He will become more agile and sure-footed and the problem is almost certain to go away.

Appropriate farriery can help. Shortening the toes can quicken the 'break-over' so the horse can pick his forefeet up in less time – therefore avoiding his hind feet. However, farriers can differ in their theories on this – some might

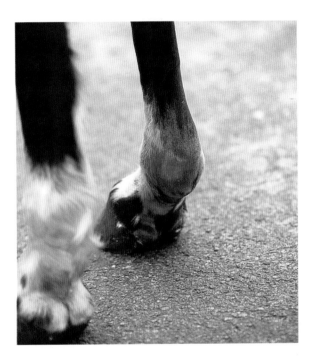

shorten the hind toes to reduce the chance of their contact with the front feet. Setting back the hind shoes and rolling or squaring the toes could also be considered. The use of over-reach or bell boots on the front feet can help avoid injury but many do not fit well and can rub the pasterns. Many models of boots are just too long and can even be a cause of the horse tripping in the first place. As a temporary measure, however, they may be advisable and cutting them shorter may help.

RELATED AREAS OF IMPROVEMENT   **63**   **72**   **87**   137

91 Increasing your horse's suppleness

Nearly all horses have a soft, 'easy' side and a stiffer, less compliant side and may be right or left 'sided' just as we are right and left handed. Theories abound on why horses are like this. Some believe that it is the way the foetus lay in the womb, others put it down to the traditional practice of always handling horses from the left, so most are more supple to the left. Today it should be common practice to handle horses equally from both sides. However, foals seem to show preferences from their early days – so my feeling is that it is genetic, like us being right or left handed.

Horse stiff on one side

A horse being stiff on one side is not a fault of the rider unless nothing is done about it. It is surprising how many people actually avoid working on the stiffer side because the horse doesn't like it and they find it difficult. Consequently, the horse's muscle development is all one-sided and his performance on his stiff side gets worse.

What can I do?

The answer is clearly to work the horse at least evenly on both sides and my inclination is to work slightly more on the stiff side or rein. However – remember that working on the stiffer side will be harder for the horse, so allow regular rest periods to avoid strains. Develop a schooling programme for your horse and keep a careful check from a knowledgeable eye on his physical condition and development.

92 Improving turns and circles

The correct position for the rider when turning is to sit upright in balance with a controlled, still torso. The seat and legs should be relaxed but toned, with the inside leg well down supporting the horse strongly in his bend or circle, with a little weight on the outside seatbone. With the inside rein, ask for an inside flexion. The outside rein should allow the flexion but remain in light contact.

It is a horse's natural way to turn at speed, and especially on fairly tight bends, with his head to the outside of the bend counteracting the weight of his body which will lean into the bend. In this way he keeps his natural balance and control over his considerable half-ton weight.

Banking and motorbiking

This is a common fault which may not be actually caused by the rider but can certainly be either exacerbated or corrected by him or her. The problem for the horse, and his rider, occurs when a rider, weighing about a sixth of his own weight, is added on top.

As far as banking is concerned, this can be pretty dangerous if the rider flops and swings around. If the horse banks on a turn and the rider leans with him, all that extra weight is added to the horse's inner side – and that weight is top heavy, moving and unstable. To get under it to control and balance it, the horse goes even further into his bend, the rider slides down more, and so it gets worse.

What can I do?

To prevent a horse leaning in, simply use the same aids for a turn but exaggerate them. With the inside rein, ask for a definite inside flexion and also raise the rein a few inches, keeping it touching the neck. This will maintain the flexion so the horse finds it difficult to load the shoulder leading into the bend. It also helps to keep the forehand upright and out on the track of the bend or circle. Perhaps the most influential aid is to weight the outside seatbone, or even move the seat slightly sideways in an exaggerated case (not leaning) towards the outside.

Mental approach

A mental *and* spiritual approach

There is no doubt that you need good physical technique to be a good rider but that is only half of the requirements. The other half is the intangible but crucial input of your mind and your spirit. It is hard to define the difference between the two. The mind seems to produce our attitudes, our intellect, our logic, maybe our instincts and it controls our emotions once they arise. The spirit is something else. I think of it as producing our inner 'knowing' – our sense of whether something is right or wrong despite our education and conditioning and, surely, our bonds with people and animals. I feel that our emotions stem from our spirit which may account for the illogicality and strength of some of them.

I feel certain that our mental approach to our horses and to riding determines how the horses respond. A positive attitude will produce much better results and more enjoyment for both of you than a negative one. I have been to several of Richard Maxwell's demonstrations and am always impressed by the fact that it never seems to enter his head that the horses will not do as he wishes. He is so positive. Horses, in fact, find this a very reassuring quality.

There is absolutely nothing to be gained by pretending to be a hero and riding a horse that frightens you to death. Riding and horse ownership can be so rewarding – so why put yourself in a situation which you don't enjoy? Many riders, including professionals, become apprehensive at some stage in their riding career, particularly if they have had a bad experience – but being apprehensive is not the same as being scared, and can be overcome.

Some years ago, I bought the old Thoroughbred mare mentioned occasionally in this book. I had not ridden for two years because I had lost my nerve – I was out of practice, unfit and had lingering weaknesses from an injury. Not the best condition in which to get involved with a hot, arrogant, independent Thoroughbred who had a low opinion of humans, was known to bite, was a double handful when in season and who went like a spider. Her owner, however, said that the mare was very good with novices and would take care of me. I looked at the mare and thought that I would never be able to ride her. I rode a less challenging horse first and, apprehensively, progressed to the mare. I began to get a strange sensation that spiritually she was marking time. Shortly after I bought her, Carol Brett of Balance International met the mare. She later sent me a card which said: 'She may not give you what you expect, but you can be sure it will be what you need.'

I still have that card and often wonder how right she was. Over the months we bonded like superglue, physically, mentally and spiritually. I just knew that despite her antics and tantrums she would never hurt me. We looked out for each other – she fully restored my confidence and became my equine soulmate. And all because something was telling me that this was right, despite all practical signs to the contrary. With this story I am trying to emphasize how important it is to listen to your mind and especially your spirit in your life with horses.

First of all we are passengers, then we become riders and finally, only by adding the extra dimensions of mind and spirit, we may become horsemen.

93 Improving your confidence

No matter how frightened you are (within reason) there is a horse somewhere who will restore your confidence – and this is just what you need. If you are frightened, a lot or a little, or if you have lost your nerve, there is plenty you can do about it, including taking time. Riding horses which scare you or rushing your rehabilitation is not the way no matter what old-fashioned, gung-ho die-hards may say. Riding with confidence - at your current level - opens up whole fields of self-respect, pleasure and bonding with a horse, so go for it.

Fear of bucking

It is understandable that many riders are afraid of bucking because, along with rearing, it is one of the most effective means available to a horse of getting a rider off.

What can I do?

To try and overcome the fear that a horse may buck, have some lessons at a reputable riding school and ride as many different horses as possible – you may find one who gives little playful, joyful bucks which are relatively easy to sit to.

Use him for experience and education – the fear of a buck is often worse than the reality. However, don't push yourself beyond what you feel is right for you. Inveterate, hard buckers are the province of the professional or semi-professional rider.

Knowing effective techniques of dealing with a horse that bucks is an immense help, as is getting fit and strong and generally riding as much as you can. This all helps to build your confidence. See page 132.

If you have a horse of your own and have a problem with bucking, your best plan is to get some experienced help to, firstly, find the cause of the bucking and, secondly, to work with you to help stop it.

94 Learning to relax when riding

Tension can only adversely affect your riding. If you are tense, your muscles tighten and you often hold your breath. Muscles have to be held slightly contracted in order to have tone to, for instance, hold the torso erect, and you have to contract them to use any part of your body. The trick is to not use your muscles when you don't need them. Use them and then relax. I find many riders are very hard and tense in the hands, gripping the reins quite unnecessarily, often also finding it hard to relax the legs and seat.

Rider tense or trying too hard

I find that this is a fairly common situation. Sometimes a rider is trying so hard to achieve a particular dressage movement, or trying to impress a new teacher or onlookers, that tension creeps in. Nervousness can also cause tension.

What can I do?

Muscles cannot completely relax when riding else we would fall off. Simply think of 'de-contracting' the muscles which describes a muscle not in use, but still toned enough to keep a rider in the saddle.

Breathing is also a good idea! When done deeply and in rhythm, it relaxes the body and mind and slows the heart rate. Breathe slowly and deeply – some riders find counting helps – and you'll find it will relax you. Your horse will also appreciate it.

General relaxation techniques help to chill out your mental attitude so that being more laid-back becomes a habit. Try aromatherapy baths or meditation, yoga or listening to calming music – and play calming, uplifting music while you ride. It's great!

95 Restoring confidence after a fall

Falling off a horse is the fastest way to lose confidence and it can take some time before you feel truly safe in the saddle again. It really is a case of going back to basics and rebuilding your confidence. Not only have I had my own confidence restored, I have also helped several other people get their nerve back. It is possible – if you really want to do it. Find a competent, understanding teacher who will let you progress at your own pace, concentrating on teaching you a deep, strong and independent seat. If you have that, you are much less likely to fall off. It is the basis of all good riding.

Fear of falling off

For many people the fear of falling off, can really dent their self-confidence which in turn can have a detrimental effect on their riding.

What can I do?

The way to deal with this problem is not to stop riding, but to ride absolutely rock-solid horses that know their jobs and will, if you ask them, just plod round in walk until even you want to trot! This may be a friend's horse, a riding school gem or a loan horse – wherever he comes from, he will be the answer to your fear.

Just being around horses and handling them can help to build your confidence as well as building a rapport with the horse you ride. Watching and familiarizing yourself with a horse's actions and reactions from the ground can help tremendously when you are in the saddle.

Remember, riding is a risky sport so it is wise to take reasonable steps to protect yourself. Invest in a hard hat which complies with the latest safety standards and take the time to get it fitted by a qualified fitter. A loose hat is as good as wearing no hat. A body protector is another wise investment –

modern designs are much less cumbersome than the original ones on the market and are now extremely light and breathable. Again, have it properly fitted and opt for the latest safety standard. Wear stout shoes or suitable footwear made for riding. Rubber or plastic riding boots offer little

protection and do not mould with your feet, ankles and legs – in fact they can make them ache because they do not help achieve a good leg position. Leather is better, ideally long boots but jodhpur boots plus chaps (leather or synthetic) are also quite good enough.

96 Developing empathy

I gave a lot of thought to the inclusion of this fault. Surely if a person has no empathy with a horse he or she should not be riding? Empathy is the ability to mentally put yourself in someone else's place, in this case your horse, to really imagine his situation and so to understand him and his feelings. Mammals all have the same basic physiological equipment. A cut with a whip hurts our horse as much as it would hurt us. To people who are whip-happy, I say – before you hit your horse, hit yourself with the whip just as hard as you were going to hit him, and then see if you can still do it.

Lack of empathy

The picture on the right shows this beautifully. Without understanding your horse you can never ride in real harmony with him and could end up blaming him for 'bad behaviour' which may have a perfectly reasonable cause but of which you are ignorant. This rider would be lucky to avoid elimination.

What can I do?

Can one develop empathy if it is missing? I believe you can if you really want to and keep your mind and eyes open to the animal in front of you. Technical learning, both equitation and care and management, are vital, of course, and it helps greatly if you constantly imagine that you are on the receiving end of your treatment of your horse. What an attitude adjuster that turns out to be! Be imaginative, too – if you were a horse, what would you do to get through to a human that your saddle hurt?

Sometimes, people just don't get on with a particular horse. It is important to have a horse you can bond with, love and respect. If people are unhappy in relationships, they usually end, and this is certainly a relationship but one in which the horse

has no choice. It's up to you. I believe empathy can come with knowledge, will and imagination. Also remember that there are an awful lot of hard-

bitten people in the horse world – don't let them colour your feelings but think for yourself. Never allow anything that goes against your conscience.

97 Using the whip fairly

A whip should be used as a support to the aids. It is true that some horses do not try if the rider does not have a whip and just carrying one produces active gaits, concentration and a co-operative attitude. With these horses, there is usually no need to use the whip on the horse at all – just waving it down their side or tapping your own leg works wonders.

Inability to use the whip correctly

What a strange topic to put in a section on the mental approach to riding! Why is it here? Because there is so much abuse of the whip and so many horses are whip shy. Once a horse has been beaten up or even hit once unfairly, he will never get over it – even with a different rider who only uses it as a guide. Some horses just won't tolerate a rider even carrying a whip, but work perfectly willingly otherwise.

What can I do?

I know that many modern and natural trainers abhor whips, and I, too, abhor the common, incorrect, unfair and unjustified use of the whip. But I sometimes carry a schooling whip if a particular horse is ignoring my leg aids, and touch him with it as a reminder or, if strictly necessary, tap or flick him in support of my leg. None of these hurt because I do it to myself to demonstrate. This is not abuse, but fair discipline under the circumstances prevailing in our world.

98 Developing your riding knowledge

A lack of confidence can stem from a lack of confidence in your own knowledge, and a sharp horse will soon take advantage. This topic is closely linked to discipline and using the whip. Unfortunately, herd society being what it is and still being instinctive in our horses, sometimes horses do have to be disciplined, as in a herd, or they do unacceptable things to other members of their herd – us. Horses, though, are big, strong animals who will easily win a straight battle of strength with a human.

Lack of confidence allowing misbehaviour

Sometimes a rider can be fit and strong, with the knowledge to deal with a problem, but dare not apply the requisite aids through fear of the horse's reaction. Harsh treatment never solves the problem and usually makes it worse.

What can I do?

The rider should remember that most 'naughty' horses are bullies and most bullies back down under perceived strength. Riding through the problem just once or twice, can make an amazing difference to a horse's entire attitude. By working with a sympathetic instructor, many problems can be worked through calmly and methodically without instigating an argument between horse and rider.

You need to ensure you are fit and strong enough to ride well. Riding can be very tiring because you are using muscles which you don't use all the time and it really helps to do some appropriate ground exercises at the gym or at home. Building up fitness and strength is part of your task – the other is learning from a supportive teacher how to cope with various misbehaviours.

99 Improving your concentration

The human brain is capable of concentrating for about 25 minutes without a break, the horse can probably concentrate for much less time. Therefore, keep your schooling sessions short, centre your mind and relax. A schooling session with your horse of 20 to 30 minutes, three times a week is enough. Even within this period, it is advisable to work for just a few minutes at a time, praise the horse and have a little break and a stretch when he's achieved something good, then start again.

Lack of concentration

This is more likely to occur when schooling alone in a manège, and probably for too long, and your mind starts to wander, particularly if you have worries. Half-hour sessions are enough, with frequent breaks.

What can I do?

When having a lesson, a wise teacher will give you frequent breaks without wasting the time for which you are paying. During them, you can chat about technique or your horse and then start again, without stressing or boring you or your horse. Hacking out is quite different – some degree of concentration has to be maintained for safety, but it gives both the horse and rider the opportunity to mentally relax and enjoy themselves.

One way of centreing your mind is to think ahead about what you are doing. Of course, you have to live in the moment when communicating with your horse, but have on the periphery of your concentration your next move or aim. A lot of schooling and riding errors occur because the rider does not plan a few strides ahead or warn the horse early enough of what is coming next.

If you've had a really bad day and are just too stressed out or not in the mood for schooling, consider the fact that you are unlikely to do a good job of it and could distract or confuse your horse and so be counter-productive. Leave it for another day, go for a hack or simply go home and chill out.

100 Developing your breathing techniques

Of course our bodies breathe when they have to. Breathing is one of those semi-voluntarily controlled activities – we can start or stop breathing and speed up or slow down our rate to some extent, but when we are asleep or are unconscious we don't have to worry about it as our bodies take over. Breathing rhythmically and reasonably deeply is not only beneficial for our general health, but it also helps us to relax. Parts of meditation lessons include instruction on different breathing techniques, for instance, and breathing and control are important parts of Pilates and yoga, and other modalities.

Forgetting to breathe

Breathing on a horse is usually curtailed when a rider is trying (too) hard or having a problem. Tension takes over and we often hold our breath. If you can get into the habit of quite often breathing in time with your horse's rhythm you will find that it helps your relaxation and concentration. One very effective technique I learned years ago for helping to subtly slow down a horse was to breathe a little more slowly than his rhythm.

What can I do?

The classical posture of a slightly expanded chest, shoulders back and down and breastbone up enlarges the volume of the lungs and allows in more air. When you stop for a break, breathe out and in quite deeply, but as fast as your body dictates, until you get your breath back. Physical activity increases your rate and depth of breathing, so don't over do it.

Working in a dusty manège or environment with both you and your horse's air intake increased will not do either of you any good at all. Avoid it if you can.

Final thoughts

Everyone has room for improvement in their riding. I hope that you have found a few techniques, at least, in this book to help you. As you'll be aware now, my favoured way of riding is traditional classical with a heavy Portuguese/old French bias. From my experiences and observations, I feel that this is the best method, especially as it transfers to jumping so well and even racing. When I first take on new clients, I give them a short recommended reading list of classical titles to get them started. Visit www.susanmcbane.com for details.

An ideal organisation for classical riding enthusiasts is The Classical Riding Club, now international and founded by teacher, trainer and author Sylvia Loch. It is based at Eden Hall, Kelso, Roxburghshire, Scotland, TD5 7QD. Or visit www.classicalriding.co.uk Another group for the thinking horseman and woman is The Equine Behaviour Forum, which I co-founded with the late Dr Moyra Williams in 1978. It is based at Carmel Cottage, 50 Marsh House Lane, Over Darwen, Lancashire, England, BB3 3JB, you can visit its website at www.gla.ac.uk/External/EBF/

I should like to acknowledge posthumously my two main classical trainers, the first being Percy Collins, who taught me as a child for 11 years until he retired. His background was the great British army equitation school, Weedon, where he absorbed a major influence from its French equivalent at Saumur. I then rode in various other ways, never being really happy, until I came across the controversial and volatile French-speaking Belgian, Dési Lorent, in the 1980s. He studied over 20 years with probably the greatest classical rider of the 20th century, the Portuguese maestro Nuño Oliveira. My present teacher, Sheila Myers of the Lakeland Riding Centre, Flookburgh, Cumbria, teaches classical principles with the guidance of French classical rider, Georges Dewez, who is based in Wales and with whom I also sometimes have lessons. You can visit their respective websites at www.lakes-riding.co.uk and www.carregdressage.co.uk.

Riding is not easy but it is an exhilarating pursuit when you get it right, and I believe that goes for the horses too. For those in danger of trying too hard and forgetting to enjoy it, I leave you with this thought:

Don't aim for perfection – be happy with excellence.
This leaves you room to be human, and equine.

Acknowledgments

I should like to thank Tracy Lloyd-Webster and her bay dressage horse, Cyril The Squirrel, and Karen Smith with her 'cheeky chestnut', Jack, who all worked and modelled for several hours with great patience for most of the photographs in this book, mainly being asked to do things wrongly which is not easy when you're used to doing them right. Julie is also to be thanked for putting her manège at our disposal, and therefore out of use, for a whole day. At the other end of the country, I am always thankful to be able to work with such a professional editorial and design team as David & Charles are fortunate to have in Jane, Sue, Sarah and Shona who get just as involved in a book as its author. Books really are a team effort.

Index

Index

Picture acknowledgments

All photography by NEIL HEPWORTH except the following:
Martin Avery (courtesy Georges Dewez): opp title page
David & Charles/Kit Houghton: pp 17, 87, 91(btm left)
Kit Houghton: pp 18, 20, 21, 22, 52, 60, 94, 121, 122, 124, 134, 135, 136, 137, 142, 144

Horsepix: pp 41, 77, 89, 90, 110, 123, 126, 129, 130, 131, 132, 133
David & Charles/Bob Atkins: pp 98, 99, 91, 147, 148
Louis Lesko/Corbis: front cover
Line artwork on page 40 by Sally Alexander